A Diff*erent View*

Of the World

*Spiritual Perspective and Understanding
for our Current Times*

Dr. Kevin T. Adam

ISBN-13: 978-1496014504

ISBN-10: 1496014502

About Kevin

My exploration into the spiritual realms began close to 40 years ago. This exploration began with reading Carlos Castaneda's *Tales of Power* in 1975 and still continues today.

My path hasn't been a straight one, and I've learned many perspectives from a large variety of sources. After reading all of Castaneda's books, I moved on to study astral projection and psychic development. In the mid- to late 1980's, I became interested in auras and spiritual energy fields, and that led me to purchase Barbara Brennan's *Hands of Light*.

At the same time, and into the early 1990's, I studied several audio programs in the series by Jonathan Parker called *In Search of Enlightenment*. These programs were very instrumental in helping me to develop spiritual understanding and perception through guided meditations.

Also in 1990, while at chiropractic college, I learned about Eckankar – Religion of the Light and Sound of God. I became a member of Eckankar, and stayed a member until about 2000. Early in my Eckankar membership, I learned about Reiki, and had my Reiki 1 attunement in 1991.

Throughout all of this, and in the years that followed, I continued meditating, honing my spiritual senses, and increasing my spiritual capacity. I worked with energy healing and became aware of problems outside our normal perceptions – then learned how to solve those problems. Problems such as energy imbalances, accumulated negative energy, damage to the body's spiritual energy system (the chakras, which I'll describe later), and even problems caused by other – mainly negative – entities.

By "entities" I mean such things as ghosts, dark angels (demons), ancient sorcerers, and even dark archangels. I learned that I could solve almost all of the problems created by these entities, and have been doing so for over 20 years. And, while doing that, I also helped some people to grow spiritually.

All of these experiences led me to where I am today – a spiritual teacher able to share important spiritual perspectives while also working to heal energy fields, balance soul energy, and clear negative entities when it's needed and spiritually right.

My hope is that the perspectives I've learned over these decades can help you to grow faster, and to go further spiritually than you could have gone before reading this book. A significant change is on the horizon, and having more people able to understand that change and take action will benefit all humankind and the Earth. Thank you for joining me on this journey.

Introduction

One of the constants in this universe is *change*. Everything is in constant motion. *Nothing* stays the same. That includes each and every one of us, the planet we live on, and even the entire cosmos. You may wonder why this is important to you, as the reader. The reason is simple: each moment of change creates an opportunity for spiritual growth.

What does it mean to be *spiritual?* To me, being spiritual starts with the understanding that there is more to us, as beings, and to the cosmos, as our home, than we can perceive with our physical senses.

Once we at least believe there is more, we learn to perceive and understand the deeper truths that are a natural part of us and our universe. With an open mind we learn to explore; we learn to question. We learn that making the right choices is better for us and for everyone around us. We develop the strength to stand behind our convictions, regardless of what anyone else in the world may say or believe. We learn to accept that there is at least some truth in our perspectives.

We each have our own view of the world. And no one's world view is 100% right. Each of us has pieces of whatever may be the ultimate truth – assuming, of course, that there is an "ultimate" truth.

What I'm offering here is my view of the world. I have no direct proof of anything I've written in this book. These thoughts come from experience, observation, and from realizations I've had while contemplating these topics.

Generally, I'll present these ideas as certainty. Some of

these ideas may even be correct in an absolute sense, although my point of view will no doubt change as it evolves. However, there may be things in these pages that others can learn from. It's my hope that, in presenting the ideas in this book, I can help some others make at least one positive step forward.

When enough of us have taken a sufficient number of small steps, we'll arrive at a tipping point – the point from which harmony between each other, and between us and the world, can naturally emerge. So let's take of few of those steps together.

Dr. Kevin T. Adam

The world as it appears

Our world certainly appears chaotic. Events seem predominantly random. There sometimes appears to be no real order, and no real sense to events that happen in this world. Despite those appearances, there are two primary driving forces for events in this world.

The first of these is *choice*. Every choice made by every person on the planet has some consequence. The sum total of all these choices and their consequences (combined with the effects of the second force, which we'll get to momentarily) results in all the events that happen throughout the world at each moment. In a sense, that means we all, collectively, co-create each moment in our existence.

Even though we may not realize it, our choices have repercussions we may not know about. To illustrate this, let's say that, for whatever odd reasons, I choose to drive a crane out into a desert area with boulders and foothills. I find a boulder I like and hook it up to the crane because I want to drop it from 30 feet up.

Once I have the boulder strapped to the crane, I hoist it up and let it fly. It slams the ground with a big boom! and I can really feel the ground shake. The vibrations that I feel continue to travel – maybe a mile or more – to a small hill with a lot of rocks. Those rocks are unstable, and the vibrations from my boulder are just enough to break them loose and cause a rockslide.
The rocks from the hillside crash down with a huge rumble... crushing two hikers out for a walk in nature.

In that instance, my actions had fatal consequences. I didn't know that would happen, and I may never even know that it *did* happen – but I'm still responsible. Our choices are like that; there are effects that ripple out from them and cause more effects. This is why, as aware spiritual beings, we need to make the best and most positive choices we can. Our choices make changes.

This means that we are collectively responsible for the world as it is today. The responsibility of each individual, however, is limited to the consequences that arise from each choice we make as an individual. This means, very specifically, that I'm not *individually* responsible for anyone else's choices or the consequences created as a result of *their* choices. What I *am* responsible for as an individual is every result that arises from my personal choices, *plus* my responses to the consequences of all the choices made by other people that have an effect on my life.

You may have heard other spiritual teachers say that each of us creates our own life. I believe this to be often misunderstood, and it fails to take into account one simple thing: that there is in fact an *objective* reality. What is *subjective* is our perception of that reality and the events that happen within it.

As an example, let's choose the Rocky Mountains. Those mountains don't exist because we choose to see them, as would be the case if all reality was subjective. Simply put, the Rocky Mountains exist whether or not I believe they exist, and whether or not I or anyone else have ever seen them. They're real; they exist. That's an *objective* reality.

What's *subjective* about the Rocky Mountains is the distinct way each of us perceives them, and how each of us feels about them. If you and I are both looking at the Rocky Mountains, what I notice will be different than what you notice. What I find beautiful you may not, and vice versa. Our *subjective* experiences could be very different, even though we're looking at the same physical mountain and the same *objective* reality.

This is important because I firmly believe it's counterproductive for anyone to walk around thinking they're responsible for everything in their life and everything they see happening around them. It's perceptually incorrect, it's overwhelming, and it can waste time and energy trying to correct things that aren't our concern or responsibility.

That does *not* mean, however, that it's spiritually acceptable to ignore things you learn about that are outside your direct circle of influence. Once you learn about something, it's moved into your circle of awareness, and this presents you with a choice: to embrace it and to try and make a positive difference, or to let it be and let others take personal responsibility for that situation.

To illustrate this with a simple example, let's look at something very common: water. We all use it, we all drink it, and many people don't pay much attention to it in our everyday American lives. Let's look at this from an individual's point of view; specifically, an individual named Jack.

Just like most Americans, Jack uses and drinks water every day, not really thinking much about it because it's always been there. Now let's say that Jack went to visit his friend Jill, and they watched TV. Jill happens to be passionate about the environment, so she put on a documentary about water that Jack had never seen. In that documentary, the filmmakers identify fresh water as a dwindling resource and something that may be much harder to get if we keep wasting water in the way that many people tend to.

Jack, learning this information, has two basic choices: 1) To think, "Well, that's interesting," and keep on doing things the way he has been, or 2) Realize from the documentary that his actions affect others, and that his choices about water have been a part of the growing problem.

Now that Jack is aware of the growing water problem in this world, this problem has moved into his personal spiritual sphere of awareness. His actions relating to water have now become his spiritual responsibility. He may choose to ignore his responsibility, or he can take action. The choice is his. One of those choices, however, is better than the other from a spiritual perspective.

Now that we've introduced the choices we make as a driving force in the events around us, let's cover the second of these driving forces: *physics*.

Physics

As you probably already know, the Laws of Physics determine how things work in this world and beyond. This applies to all physical interactions, which include many of the results, or consequences, of our decisions. This is probably fairly obvious, but it's important because you need to understand that no amount of wishing on our part can overcome these physical laws.

Therefore, any actions you take will have reactions *that are limited to what is possible within any given situation*. This means you need to reasonably anticipate the most likely results. For example, if you're playing catch with a friend, it's reasonable to anticipate that the ball will initially go up, then land somewhere else. It would not, however, be reasonable to anticipate that the ball will reach orbit simply because you threw it.

All of our choices are like this; they all have a possible set of consequences that range from most likely to nearly impossible. And while we can't be absolutely certain of any specific reaction or consequence, it's critical to consider the most likely consequences when we make our choices. Typically, the best choice will lead to the most positive outcome and provide a positive outcome for others as well. Consistently choosing your actions with this level of outcome in mind will help you make the best possible choice – even though it may not be the choice that meets *your* preference.

The importance of Consciousness

I am certain that this is a created universe. My view on that, however, is probably somewhat different from what most religions seem to teach. Many religions give God human form and qualities – and that's a limitation on God that simply doesn't apply. The creator of this universe isn't angry, vengeful, or directing every action in our daily lives. This point of view comes only from organized religions.

In this book, God and the Creator are the same, as in conventional religions. However, my perspective on our creator will be different from the point of view you'll find in most religions. Keep that in mind since I'll be sharing more about our creator in a later section. Now let's cover the importance of *consciousness*.

The traditional definition of consciousness is awareness of one's own existence. I consider that a *faculty* of consciousness and not a full definition of it. I see consciousness as more than being simply self-aware. To me, self-awareness as an individual is *sentience,* but consciousness runs deeper. Consciousness is the self-aware energy that is the basis for all life. It's the energy that separates a living, breathing human from a corpse. That energy has been a part of our universe since its very beginning.

To create our universe, our creator took a specific quantity of energy (more detail on this coming later), and infused that energy with consciousness to create this universe.

This consciousness fills the entire universe, and it's in us too. That consciousness was created to evolve. It's designed to *grow.* I call this all-pervasive consciousness the Evolving

Divine Consciousness (EDC). Each one of us has the energy of this Evolving Divine Consciousness within us, and it's this consciousness that is the reason we experience personal and spiritual growth.

As each of us grows, *so does the entire Evolving Divine Consciousness*. Despite all appearances of separation and isolation, we are all formed from *one* consciousness; in fact, the EDC is the *only* consciousness in our universe. So, the consciousness of each and every one of us comes from the same exact source.

From this perspective, anything any of us do that hurts others, or hurts the planet, *hurts us too at the same time*. If we accept this could be true, what can we do with that information?

One choice is to disbelieve it and disregard it. You can continue living your life as you have been, holding onto your beliefs whether or not they may be wrong. Or, you can choose to put aside any beliefs that conflict with this point of view. You can embrace the idea that we all share the same origin. If you do this, and truly internalize what this means, then you'll be able to live your life in harmony with the earth and its inhabitants, and live in harmony with natural and spiritual law.

Such a life is our true birthright; it's genuinely the highest expression of our true nature. When you realize the significance of this choice, you'll understand that it's time to stop killing our home planet with pollution, environmental destruction, chemicals, microwaves, and all the other poisons we've spread across the planet.

By making this choice, you'll come to accept and understand that harmony between us, and between us and nature, is the highest form of life and existence we can have on the Earth.

God and Creation

In the beginning, our universe started out as *potential space* – like the soap film over the opening in a child's bubble wand. This universe was created by God adding consciousness to a specific quantity of physical energy. Adding the consciousness was just like blowing into the wand to make a bubble. In the case of our universe, this created an expanding, three-dimensional space.

Adding consciousness gave the energy form – thus physical matter was created. And that's the reason why, in our universe, energy is neither created nor destroyed – it's only changed. Consciousness was injected into a finite, *specific* quantity of energy.

God created this universe with a specific set of physics that we generally call "physical laws." Mostly, those physical laws cover things we can see, measure, and interact with. But there are things in our universe that we don't perceive with our physical senses; things we can't scientifically measure.

Anything that we believe exists that we don't physically see, can't measure, and can't interact with on a physical level are things we often call "spiritual." Things like "chi" - the energy in our bodies that gives us life, or ghosts, auras, chakras, and even the energy harnessed through faith and prayer.

What's important to recognize is that spirituality is simply a form of science that interacts with our consciousness, rather than with our physical world. The same rules created with the universe still apply, but interacting with "spiritual" science comes through our consciousness and not our physical senses. Even though these forces may seem mystical or magical, they're actually a science that we are now beginning to understand, along with its role in our spiritual growth.

The Big Bang

If this universe is created, what about the Big Bang? Well, the Big Bang did happen, but the cause of the Big Bang – which is currently unknown to science – was simply adding the energy of consciousness to the physical energy that forms our universe. We see most of the combined energy as matter, and experience some of it as light, heat, and vibration. This leaves a lot of energy and matter that we don't directly perceive, and current science calls these *dark matter* and *dark energy*. Dark matter is still physical matter, although it doesn't reflect light so we don't see it.

Dark energy – which pervades our entire universe – is the *physical manifestation of the Evolving Divine Consciousness.* Scientifically, dark energy is considered to be diffusely and uniformly spread out throughout the universe. Some scientists think dark energy is the reason that the universe seems to not only be expanding, but expanding faster as the universe gets older.

Dark energy can't be directly observed, and that's completely understandable if you look at it from a spiritual point of view – since spiritual energy is also invisible to our physical senses and virtually every form of current science.

If we accept that the Big Bang happened when physical energy was infused with the energy of consciousness, it's fairly simple to see how consciousness would be diffusely and uniformly spread out through space, just as dark energy is. Since neither can be directly observed, and

16

they're both spread out the same way, it's reasonable to postulate that dark energy and the EDC could at least interrelate, or indeed be one and the same.

Let's go a step further with this. The Big Bang had to happen *somewhere* in the universe. If you go to that exact location, you'll find an enormous black hole that is larger than the super-massive black holes at the centers of galaxies. This is the exact spot where consciousness was injected into the specific quantity of energy that created our universe. It's also a type of gateway that leads to a universe outside of ours, and this is the universe from which ours was created. This outer universe is the home of God, and it's the realm where energy is created.

Time

To most of us, time seems to be a measure of everything that occurs around us. It allows us to quantify our memories and plan our futures. It seems to be in constant movement, turning the present into the past and the future into the present. Despite that appearance, time is none of those things.

The true essence of time is that it exists in only one single moment – one single instant. That instant is *NOW*. This can be a bit confusing, since each moment seems to flow into the next in an endless series of moments that connect to each other. This seeming flow is what we call time, and it's also how we measure time.

The confusion comes from equating "moment" with some portion of "second." With that basic premise, then one moment seems to flow into another just as one second passes to the next. This basic premise, however, is wrong. The one moment that exists in this Universe has no duration – it's unrelated to our description of time, and *it doesn't move or change*. It's a fixed point of time, and it's the *events* in the universe that flow and change, one into the other.

These changing events have an order, or sequence. We relate those events to the moment they happen, and that's why we think of time as following a flow of moments - from the past... to now... to the future. So, what we call "time" is only a description of the *changes* we see around us.

As things change around us, we naturally remember them in sequence. The terms past, present, and future help make it easier to communicate about the events we see or anticipate. The greatest confusion has come from believing that these terms – which make communicating easier – are accurate descriptions about what is really happening when they're actually not.

Past, present and future describe our perception of time, but not the reality of it. Naming something makes it tangible, and by describing something as "past" we begin to make the past concrete in our minds. After all, if we can remember it, shouldn't there be a chance we can do it over again, or relive it?

Thinking like this creates confusion, and has led some to think that time travel could be real. Those earlier "times" did exist as we lived them, and they exist in our memories. All that exists of those moments now, in the present, is our memory of them. Nothing about those past moments still exists in our moment of "now." Past moments existed only as a static instant; a specific arrangement of the universe at that exact moment. Once *anything* changed, that "present moment" became "the past," and that moment is permanently gone from this universe.

The events we experience in sequence give the *illusion* that time flows around us. It gives the illusion that the past is still out there somewhere, and we may some day be able to revisit it. But that's not true. The past doesn't exist. Only our memories of it exist. The flow from past to future exists only as a reference point for our conscious mind.

It also gives the illusion that the universe has a specific, definable age. What we call the "age" of the universe is nothing more than a handy description to make these changes understandable, and put them in a context that matches our perception to our memory. In other words, we say the universe is 13.7 billion years old so we can put the changes we've observed within the universe into an order that matches how we perceive those changes – as a flow of time.

One could now ask: is the universe *really* 13.7 billion years old, or does it all exist in one infinite moment? The answer is both – sort of. You see, those 13.7 billion years simply describe the flow of change in the universe. Even though all changes happen in the same moment, *those changes haven't happened all at once.* It's been a progression, a sequence of change, a flow of changes that we assign reference points to and call time.

The past is nothing more than our description of a previous state in which the universe existed. It's not "there" to travel back to, and there is no possibility of rewinding all the changes in the universe to a previous state to re-create the "past." I suppose some sci-fi writers won't like that very much.

So what about the future? What we think of as the "future" comes from our cognitive capacity to anticipate; to plan. We anticipate time moving forward until we get to a specific day or time, and we plan an event or make an appointment. This verifies our notion that the future will exist; it's just "later."

Even though the future doesn't even exist, we still seem to get there because of our inherent capacity to anticipate. That makes it difficult to break free from the idea of time being a flow. It can also make us think that all times are present. However, it's only memory or anticipation that makes us think there are different times at all.

Only one moment has ever existed, and that moment is NOW. In this universe, what changes is not time; it's *conditions* that change. We mark those changes as time passing. But it's actually not time "passing." It's actually the universe evolving and changing within one single, all-encompassing moment.

It's important to remember that it's only *one* moment, and not a series of moments strung together like we string seconds together. Thinking of moments like seconds makes it very difficult to understand how there can be just one "now" in the universe. And, everything that has occurred to this point has occurred in sequence necessary to arrive at the point we call "now."

There is one important thing I'd like to mention about "the future." It's not set, or predetermined. It's the product of two things: our collective choices that generate action, and physics. Our "future" is a vast collection of probabilities, and our actions in every moment, along with the laws of physics, bring events from "probable" to "happen." The events that make up our Now, and become our past, mainly result from the actions we take and how those actions occur according to physics.

This means every choice we make forms the Now, and choosing one action over another creates a different Now than would have existed had a different choice been made. It's in this way that seemingly small choices can steer your entire life in one direction instead of another.

A great example of this came from my father-in-law. He told me that in high school, he and a friend went to a career day, and they were both interested in the Air Force. But the Air Force line was too long and they didn't want to wait, so they went to the Army table instead since there was a short line – and he enlisted in the Army for a number of years during the Vietnam War. A seemingly small decision that most likely steered his entire life in a much different direction than if he'd gone into the Air Force.

I'd like to mention one additional point relating to choices: While small decisions can have enormous impact, it's unwise and unnecessary to agonize over every tiny decision. Simply make the best decision you can with the information you have, and let things unfold from there.

A side note about time travel

I want to add this section as a personal indulgence, and to put straight some erroneous ideas about time travel you'll "learn" about from scientists, or see presented in science fiction shows and movies.

Many of them get it wrong because their understanding of time is flawed. Scientists and science fiction writers sometimes start with incorrect assumptions, so they commonly end up with incorrect conclusions. I'd like to put one idea permanently to rest: Physical time travel to the past cannot be achieved in this universe. It's impossible.

That's simply because the past, as I wrote earlier, doesn't exist. What we call "the past" is nothing more than our memories as things change around us. Our memories make it appear as though the past exists, when the only true time in the universe is this very moment. Since the past doesn't exist, it would have to be re-created within this moment – the NOW. That would mean effectively rewinding every change in the universe until reaching the desired past moment. That is clearly not possible. That's why, in all the history of this universe, no one ever has or ever will travel to the past.

Time travel to "the future," however, is "built in" to the

structure of our universe. "The future" doesn't exist yet, and can't exist in the moment of NOW. But Einstein's theory of general relativity clearly demonstrates that moving at faster speeds affects how we observe time. That may seem to be complicated, but it's actually a very easy concept within the framework I'm explaining.

Traveling to the "future" is as simple as *speeding up the pace of change*. It's just like driving on a road, instead of walking it. You can drive a mile of highway in a little under a minute, but walking that same mile could take 15 to 20 minutes. By driving, *you've compressed 15 minutes of travel into one minute*. At the end of that mile of driving, you're 15 minutes into the future of someone walking that mile.

So, even though time only "speeds up" a tiny amount at the physical speeds we can currently reach, moving faster through the universe still creates a type of "time travel" into the future. This effect, called "time dilation," will become more of a factor when we eventually begin traveling at interstellar speeds.

The spiritual structure
of the universe

When our universe was created, as I described in a previous section, it was created with a specific physical form and a particular set of physical laws. It was also created with a specific spiritual form, and a particular set of spiritual laws. I'll be sharing more information on spiritual law later, so this section will focus on explaining the spiritual structure of our universe.

As I mentioned, the Big Bang was set in motion by infusing a specific spiritual consciousness into the energy that forms our universe. This consciousness is singular – there is only one. That consciousness was created and designed to evolve and grow. In order to grow as effectively and efficiently as possible, it separated out numerous small, holographic pieces of itself to create *souls* (if you're not familiar with holograms, each little individual piece of a hologram contains the entire picture- just a smaller version of it). The process was very specifically designed, and resulted in a specific spiritual structure.

As you may remember, I call the single, universal consciousness that permeates our entire universe the Evolving Divine Consciousness (EDC). This consciousness split off smaller pieces that we call souls, but there are a few "steps" in between the EDC and our soul. The end of these steps is *individuation;* or the part of the soul that makes us who we are in and beyond our physical bodies. Next, I'll tell you about the steps between the EDC and us.

Each physical galaxy in our universe has a piece of consciousness directly extended from the EDC. This "galactic" consciousness is split further, with a smaller piece going to each star system. However, the star systems that have sentient life get a "bigger" piece of consciousness. Each "planetary," or star system consciousness, breaks down even further. The planetary consciousness divides into Spirit groups, and these Spirit groups divide into individual Souls, which inhabit bodies. Looked at it in this way, it's easy to see that the consciousness that fills our universe is the source for every single soul throughout the entire universe. That's the true meaning of "we're all One."

Before I get further into the structure of the Spirit groups, I'd like to explain a bit more about the Planetary consciousness.

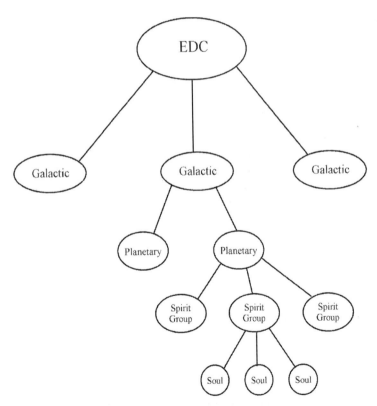

This image shows the individuation process the EDC went through to create each individual soul.

Each planet in every star system in every galaxy has a planetary consciousness. However, planets with sentient life have a bigger "piece" of the galactic consciousness. This planetary consciousness is a true, individualized being that any of us can communicate with. There have also been times in human history when the planetary consciousness has communicated with us directly. One such time that we've all heard about was the person we know as Jesus.

Jesus, for the first 30 years of his life, was an ordinary human, although he was a human with a very old and wise soul. As a wise soul, he knew he was there to prepare the way for the planetary consciousness to speak through him for a short time.

Around the time of his 30th birthday, the planetary consciousness manifested in Jesus and began to speak to the world through him. This began the time of Jesus performing miracles. It's when he taught sermons, and taught about our spiritual role in the world – explaining these things in terms understandable to the people of the time.

After sharing the essential messages, the planetary consciousness withdrew from his body during the time of Jesus' crucifixion. That's the reason for Jesus' statements about being forsaken by God during his crucifixion. The planetary consciousness had to leave before Jesus' physical body died, and that left his body with only his original soul in place.

He wasn't forsaken in a spiritual sense, but the planetary consciousness did have to leave Jesus' body before he died so that the part of his soul inhabiting the physical body would be free to rejoin his Soul in the Spirit group. That change is why he felt the way he did during a very difficult experience.

Now, let's get to the structure of the Spirit groups.

The "anatomy" of Spirit groups

Spirit groups are an essential part of the individuation process. They're the direct source of the individual Souls that inhabit bodies. There are a few important things to know about Spirit groups and Souls. I'll focus my description on how things work here on Earth, although the process is the same everywhere else (yes, that means there is sentient life throughout this galaxy and universe). It's just easier for us as humans to understand this process from our own perspective.

Spirit groups are divided into a fairly large number of individualized, but connected, Souls. The Souls in the Spirit group exist in bodies on Earth, *but those Souls can be in bodies anywhere on Earth, or during any historical period or time frame on Earth.*

Here is an analogy that may help: Imagine a vast maze. Let's put 1000 people into that maze. Their goal is to meet in the center of that maze. But the maze is so large that there are various cities at different points in the maze. Those 1000 people are wandering the maze – and they're all part of the same Spirit group. And, to make it tougher, they don't have a map or directions, and can only navigate the maze by trial and error.

Some of them enjoy the sights and sounds, spending a lot of time immersed in the experience. Others get right to the task of finding the center of the maze, remembering their steps and learning as they go. All of them take a different route, but all have the same purpose in the end: to join together in the center of the maze.

As you've probably guessed, the maze is an attempt to describe the idea behind all the members of the same Spirit group being in different places on Earth, and existing during different time periods. Regardless of when or where on Earth you and the rest of your Spirit group are, the goal for everyone, in all the Spirit groups, is the same: to ultimately fulfill our spiritual goals by learning everything we need to in order to grow.

We bring everything we learn back to our Spirit group and our Spirit group grows, too. There is an important purpose behind this, an "ultimate" goal, so to speak, and I'll describe that goal at the end of this section.

There is one other thing that I need to mention too, and that is this: even though each of us is a Soul - a direct piece of the EDC - our *entire* soul doesn't squeeze into the confines of our physical body. Only a part of it does, and the rest stays with our Spirit group.

This means that we, in our physical bodies, have a Soul that makes us who we are, and is also connected to an even bigger part of "us" that stays with our Group. It also means that we're directly connected to others in our Spirit group, regardless of where or when they're on Earth.

This is important to understand because our personal and spiritual growth directly impacts not only us, but also our Spirit group, the planetary and galactic consciousnesses, and even the EDC. Every one of us has a part to play, and it's important that we get things right and learn what we need to. We need to do our part so the Whole can grow. Fortunately, we get more than one shot at getting it right.

Reincarnation

Reincarnation is the process we use to learn, grow, and in the end, fulfill our part in the growth of the Evolving Divine Consciousness. It's the process of our soul inhabiting different bodies at different times and in different locations. In this way, we have many experiences as humans, and that gives us a repetitive learning process. Think of it as a cycle of "re-do's," with the added benefit of making progress too.

If you think back to the section about time, you may see that all of past human history over the entire earth has been available to our souls when we need to inhabit a body. Although I'm not absolutely certain of this, I believe that, for the vast majority, there is only one body occupied by our individual soul on the Earth at any specific time.

Naturally, there could be other members of our Spirit group on the Earth at the same time as we are, but it's overall somewhat unlikely that you'll cross paths – although it does sometimes happen. If this does happen, it's often for a specific spiritual reason or lesson. But, as I mentioned, it's a relatively uncommon event.

Another aspect of reincarnation is the ability some souls have to tap into the other "parts" of their Soul – parts that inhabit different bodies at different times in different locations. I think this accounts for at least some "memories" that surface during a past-life regression. I'd say it's a quite handy ability to have since such a person could have access to more experiences than just their own as an individual. The benefits of being able to tap into other "parts" of your Soul could include being better able to handle situations that come up, and possibly learning faster and moving ahead spiritually at a faster pace.

Aside from these benefits, and the comfort of knowing that everything doesn't ride on one single trip, I don't think there is a lot of spiritually beneficial information to glean by examining past lives. Many of those issues may already be resolved, and focusing on the past takes away valuable time better used for learning in the present.

The spiritual worlds

We can see, hear, smell, and touch the physical world around us. What isn't obvious to those senses is that there are spiritual worlds around us too. One part of these spiritual worlds connects to our "local" world – Earth. The other part is shared with the entire universe, so we can think of these as "universal" spiritual worlds.

Just as we have a body here in the physical world, we have a "body" for each of the spiritual worlds too. You'll find more information about these spiritual bodies in the next chapter, after I briefly describe each of the spiritual worlds.

The "local" spiritual worlds, in a broad sense, are described below. These local worlds, often referred to as "planes," also correspond to the spiritual energy framework that's connected with our physical bodies. The "planes" are:

- the *Astral* plane
- the *Causal* plane
- the *Mental* plane
- the *Soul* plane

I'll give you a short description of each plane in this book, but you'll find many resources available if you want to investigate this further. You may also find, in your further research, that other authors divide the planes into more levels, or use different names for these planes. While the verbiage may differ, the essence of all these descriptions is the same.

The physical world, as we all know, has matter, and that matter has three predominant forms: solid, liquid, and gas.

But regardless of the form, all three of these forms have one thing in common: they're all made up of the same thing, and that one thing is energy. But – not all energy is the same.

Let's compare the energy in the physical and spiritual worlds to the color spectrum. Please understand that I'm not saying that these two systems directly relate; I'm simply using one to describe the other. The basic color spectrum is described by this anagram:

ROYGBIV

Each letter is a color, and the color relates to the *wavelength* of the light, with the R standing for Red and having the longest wavelength. The V, which stands for Violet, has the shortest wavelength. So the anagram above represents visible light from the longest to the shortest wavelength.

The physical and spiritual worlds relate in much the same way, with the difference being that it's the wavelength of the spiritual energy which gets shorter up the scale instead of the wavelength of visible light. Plus, the amount of spiritual energy increases as we move further from the physical plane. Let's look at it this way:

R	O	Y	G	B	I	V
Physical	*Astral*	*Causal*	*Mental*	*Soul*		

Because of this arrangement, it's easy to think of the planes as one flowing into the other, just like the color spectrum. However, these planes aren't arranged like the layers of an onion. Instead, all of these spiritual worlds *exist in the same space as the physical world.* In the same way that combining all the colors in the spectrum forms white light, all the Planes blend to form our world.

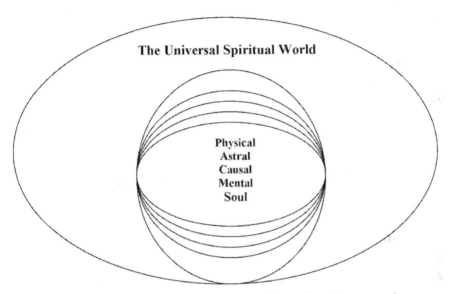

In this diagram, I'm attempting to show that the spiritual worlds exist in the same "space" as the physical world—they all inter-penetrate. The Universal Spiritual World shown above is shared with many other planets with sentient life, all of which have the same physical and spiritual structure as the Earth.

This may seem confusing, but it's not as odd as you may think. There are many things around us in our world that we can't see, and two examples are radio and TV broadcasts. The reason they're called "broadcasts" is that they're sent *everywhere.* They're not, for example, individually "beamed" to our radio or TV sets. They're broadcast everywhere, and our devices pick up the signals. In fact, if you could see radio and TV waves, you'd barely

33

see anything else because the radio and TV waves would make a permanent haze.

Well, just as we can't see TV broadcasts with just our eyes and without a TV, or hear radio with just our ears and no radio, we don't perceive the spiritual worlds with our physical senses. They're all around us, but we only perceive them when we use our *spiritual* senses – our spiritual "radios." The good news about that is this: you can learn to use your spiritual senses, even if it's not something you've done or tried before.

I'd like to mention one other point about this. While I'm describing them as separate, individual worlds, they're actually not. Much like the color spectrum, one level blends into the next. Just as red is a range of colors that become red-orange, then orange, then orange-yellow, to yellow, etc., so does each spiritual world blend into the next.

However, there is a point at which one level ends and the next begins, just like in the color spectrum. You can feel this transition point once you become accustomed to the differences at each level. With time and practice, you'll become able to feel these changes and to move your consciousness throughout the full range of the "local" spiritual worlds.

With that as a background, let's move on to describing the primary spiritual worlds attached to the Earth.

The Astral Plane

Most of us are quite familiar with the Astral plane, even if we're not aware that we are. We're familiar with it because that's where many of our dreams take place. Some of our dreams happen entirely inside our heads, and are part of the memory and information storage process. However, there are also some dreams that happen *outside* the confines of our minds. Many of those dreams take place on the Astral plane, and often involve other people that we may or may not know.

If you think about your dreams, it's easy to tell that the Astral plane is a lot like our physical world. Not *exactly* like it, but it's very similar. The main difference is in the *vibrational energy frequency* of the Astral world as compared to the physical world. This means that there is more spiritual energy on the Astral plane when compared to the physical plane.

It also means that the physics work a bit differently, and that's why seemingly odd things tend to happen in dreams. But, in general, the form and structure of the Astral plane is very much like the physical. If you're interested in specifically studying the Astral plane, then look up *astral projection*. That's a means of consciously traveling through the Astral world.

The Causal Plane

Just as vibrational frequency differentiates the physical and Astral world, so does it also differentiate the Astral from the Causal. The Causal plane resembles Earth much less than the Astral plane does. It's not formless, but forms are less fixed and more "malleable," or changeable. As you may have suspected, it's the plane where "causes" – as in "cause and effect" – happen *before* those causes manifest here.

To me, the basic "geography" of the Causal plane is more free-form and less constructed. Constructs exist here, but they're less permanent than on the physical plane and constructs tend to eventually dissipate after they've manifested on Earth. In essence, the energy for that construct has transferred from the Causal plane to the physical.

At this point, some readers may be wondering if a person can "cause" things to happen on the Causal plane (set them in motion, so to speak) and then have them manifest here on Earth. The answer is yes, but.... The "but" comes from the fact that every single event on Earth is forming our future in every moment.

If you attempt to create something at the causal level that opposes the momentum of every other choice being made on the planet, your manifestation will fail. However, it is entirely possible to create something at the causal level that *can* manifest – but it will need to be in accord with the overall direction and momentum of the energy that is already manifesting.

As you may surmise, there's little point in putting effort into manifesting something that is already forming, so I personally believe that trying to "force" something to manifest from the Causal plane is unnecessary. However, becoming aware of the events unfolding on the Causal plane can be very helpful.

This level of awareness can help you choose between different actions. With a deeper understanding of cause and effect, choosing the best course of action is much easier. This is the most effective way to "manifest" something you want – take the steps that cause it to happen. Having a deeper understanding of cause and effect can also guide your actions so you're able to take the proper steps to manifest your goals.

This understanding can also help in another less obvious way. If you learn to become aware of and consciously able to observe the Causal plane, it's also possible to see when a course of action you want to take will work *against* the overall flow of manifestation.

When this happens, your efforts will most likely meet with more roadblocks, and you'll encounter more difficulties in trying to "make" something happen. Plus, even if you do succeed, the return on your efforts will be much less. It's far better to work with the flow of manifestation and put effort into gently "steering," rather than fighting the momentum of the overall flow.

The Mental Plane

Thoughts, not surprisingly, can and do create forms on the Mental Plane. At this level, fleeting thoughts don't fully manifest – they're more like ghosts or shadows. Focused, intent thought creates forms that look very much like three-dimensional objects here on Earth. This level is often used by inventors who generate thought forms for their ideas, and those thought forms serve as a basic template for them to use as they're designing their invention.

One of the greatest at this – and one of mankind's greatest inventors – was Nikola Tesla. It was Tesla who created our electrical system and the foundation for all modern electronics. He described his process of inventing things in his autobiography, and it demonstrates mastery of the Mental Plane.

Once Tesla had an idea, he'd construct it in his mind. Since it was focused, intent thought, this also created a "working" model on the Mental Plane. He'd then imagine the device working, and would *mentally* make revisions and improvements until the function or output met his requirements – then that final version is what he'd build. That final mental design became his first physical prototype, and most of his prototypes were nearly perfect.

He had such a powerful mind that he could watch the created form on the Mental Plane perform its function, then revise that form until it was right. Every inventor works in this way to some degree, but few are able to make such a direct use of the Mental Plane.

As an observer on the Mental Plane, you'll see numerous shadowy and fleeting forms, and occasional three-dimensional forms created by others. There's not an inherent "landscape" like we see here on Earth. Form tends to be more fluid and less permanent. Naturally, you can also bring your own thought forms into creation as Tesla did, and you can use this information if you're developing an invention or process of your own.

Sometimes, other authors add a Plane between the Mental Plane and the Soul Plane, and it's often called the *Etheric* Plane. Essentially, the Etheric is the upper part of the Mental Plane, and it's simply the transition "zone" between the spiritual worlds and the three-dimensional realm of space-time. It's the "space" in which the formless begins to take shape.

The Soul Plane

The Soul Plane is a true spiritual plane, and lies somewhat "apart" from our physical space-time. Forms only exist here as a means of conveying ideas and understanding, or to help the information on the Soul Plane make sense to our limited minds. Our minds need form to learn and to grow, so there needs to be a way and a place to translate the formless into recognizable and understandable images. This takes place for us on the Soul Plane.

When you visit the Soul Plane, you'll most often encounter

people or other beings. However, there are some true "locations" as well. These locations exist as gathering places for us and for others who may visit the energy field of the Earth. All the locations have some sort of structure, which we'd call temples, and those structures are generally very bright because they're made from solidified spiritual energy.

Since all these Planes exist as a part of the Earth, each of these temples on the Soul Plane corresponds to a physical location on Earth. Most of them are in places that seem to be more "spiritual," or to have a special energy about them. That energy is most often due to the existence of the energy temple on the Soul Plane radiating through the other Planes and manifesting in our physical world.

In addition to being a gathering place, the Soul Plane is a doorway to the higher spiritual world. It's the part of our world that directly connects to the highest spiritual world. This means that the physical world we all perceive, up to and including the Soul Plane, are all a part of the Earth. It's after this point, in the world beyond the Soul Plane, that things change.

In other words, *every* planet in this universe has its own Physical, Astral, Causal, Mental, and Soul Planes. Then each world's Soul Plane is a connection to a higher Spiritual world *that is shared by every sentient planet in this universe.* This higher level spiritual world is what I call the **Universal Spiritual World.**

The Universal Spiritual World
Beyond the Soul Plane of the Earth, and all other worlds – particularly those with sentient life – exists a spiritual world that few people on Earth perceive. I call this the *Universal Spiritual World,* and it's "universal" for a good

reason: There is only one Universal Spiritual World, and the planes within it are shared throughout the entire Universe.

This means that sentient beings from the Earth, the other sentient species in our galaxy, and all the species in every other galaxy, all share this one spiritual world. The Soul plane of every planetary system with sentient life connects to this world, and we can – and often do – encounter beings of other species from across the universe when we travel in the Universal Spiritual World.

We don't generally know we're encountering species we'd call "extraterrestrial." That's because our consciousness translates the appearance of their Soul body into a form our mind can understand; for us, that's obviously the human form. This means that some of us here on Earth have indeed had an extraterrestrial encounter without even realizing it.

This spiritual world is predominantly without physical form, although temporary forms are used when they're needed to make communicating easier. The Universal Spiritual World is pure spiritual energy, but it's also stratified, like the Planes attached to Earth.

The arrangement is not exactly the same as the Planes, however. The Universal Spiritual World is arranged more like an atmosphere, which is most dense near the planet and less dense further away. In this case, though, we need to exchange air density for energy frequency.

The level of the Universal Spiritual World closest to the Soul Planes of the sentient planets has the lowest energy frequency of the Universal Spiritual World, and the spiritual energy frequency gets higher as we get further from the Soul Plane and manifested space-time (the physical universe we all live in).

I know this is a bit of a mind-bender, but the important point to take away from this is that all the sentient beings in this entire universe have access to each other through the Universal Spiritual World, and can share knowledge, perspective, and wisdom. In that way, we help each other grow and add more to the cumulative knowledge of the Evolving Divine Consciousness.

Spiritual Beings

Not every being you encounter in the Universal Spiritual World is a Soul attached to a physical body. Some of them are beings that exist *only* on spiritual planes. One example we've all heard about are angels. The natural home for angels is the Universal Spiritual World, so they naturally exist outside the limits of space-time. This also means that the same angels we know about *exist for all other sentient beings too.*

There are other types of spiritual beings as well, and all of them can interact with physical beings anywhere in the universe. Their help keeps all the inhabitants of this universe working predominantly toward the same goal. Without their help and guidance, it would be very difficult for the many trillions of different embodied Souls to learn what we specifically need to in order for the Evolving Divine Consciousness (EDC) to grow into its true form.

Each of us contributes in a very specific way to the overall growth of the EDC. More importantly, it's a contribution only we can make. Even though that may sound like a lot of pressure, I assure you it's not. Remember that we get as many opportunities to get things right as we need to. In the end, each of us *will* succeed in reaching that goal. Ultimately, we can't fail.

What's all this for?

There is a final goal for us and the evolving consciousness of this universe. If you look back to the section about creation, you'll see that the creator of this universe is outside of it. Well, just like us, that creator needs to procreate – and that's why It's creating other universes. The consciousness of each universe is designed to grow and ultimately become a distinct, self-aware, and fully formed *creator*.

After we've all done our part, and after the universe has served its purpose, the EDC will have "matured" to the point where it, too, can create universes by infusing consciousness into energy. That's a long way off from our perspective, but that is, nonetheless, our purpose and goal. That's the main reason we, as sentient beings, learn to become conscious *co-creators* – we learn that our actions have consequences, so we learn to choose the actions that will give us the result that supports the long-term goal of becoming a true creator.

The structure of Soul

It's likely that you have come across the term "aura." What I'm about to share with you may have some similarities with what you've learned in the past. However, it could conflict with what you've previously learned, or you may not be at all familiar with that term. Either way, you'll hopefully know more about our energy structure than you did before reading this chapter if this concept is new to you.

The Soul

Each one of us is more than a physical body – we truly are "more than meets the eye." In addition to our physical bodies, we all know that emotions and thoughts are a part of our "being." But our existence doesn't stop there. Our *consciousness* is the part of us that provides the spiritual energy for our physical bodies to be "alive" rather than dead. Our consciousness is our connection to the Divine, and it is the only reason our physical bodies even exist.

Our Soul is the energy framework that supports our physical body. It's the Soul connecting to and inhabiting the physical body that makes us alive and not dead. This energy framework has a structure, and that structure is called the *Human Energy Field.*

An introduction to the Human Energy Field

Our physical body is part of a complex system that we can't see with our physical eyes. Many refer to this as the "aura," but the aura is only a small part of our true energy field.

First, it's important to understand that the body doesn't generate the human energy field; instead, it's the human energy field *that is a template upon which the physical body grows.* Science tells us our bodies are the way they are because of our DNA, and that, by itself, is true. However, there's much more to this since, on its own, *DNA is powerless to grow ANYTHING.*

DNA is the physical representation of the energy "map" provided by our soul, much like the binary code which allows a computer to do many different things. This "map" is much more than a 2-dimensional representation of our true self; it's in fact a multi-layered system that works to ensure that our spiritual consciousness permeates our entire physical and spiritual being.

This essentially means that our "self," in addition to having a physical body, has spiritual bodies too. These spiritual bodies are just as real as our physical body, and, like our physical body, they also can become ill or injured. A spiritual illness or injury often manifests as an illness in the physical body. And, although it's less common, a physical illness or injury can affect the spiritual bodies, or energy field.

I know that some of this may seem odd, and we've barely touched on what I can tell you about this subject, but there are some good books available that can fill in the missing information. If you'd like to know more about this subject, check the references section at the end of the book.

A basic overview of the Human Energy Field
Essentially; the Human Energy Field is the manifested part of our Soul. It's the connection between the Divine and our physical bodies. It's also the reason we can exist in the spiritual planes because it's made up of, in essence, our spiritual bodies.

The Human Energy Field has a number of different energy "components" that, together, form the complete energy field. I'll give you a brief description of each component here, and there are many resources available with more information if you want more detailed descriptions.

The Chakra System

You've probably at least heard the word "chakra" before. The chakras are a part of the energy system for the Human Energy Field. The chakras themselves are energy vortexes, each of which both absorbs and emits energy in a particular range of frequencies. Most of the chakras exist on the front and back, and all of them connect to a central "power line" that runs through your energy field. I've seen this "power line" referred to as the "main vertical power current," and I think that's a good, descriptive name.

Most descriptions you'll see of the chakra system cover seven chakras, but there is actually an eighth chakra that has a very specific function, and there are other chakras present that we can't perceive. Here is a list of the first eight chakras and some very brief descriptions of what they affect. Please note that some of this may differ from other descriptions you may have previously read.

Chakra 1: Root Chakra

The Root chakra is our connection to the Earth energy. It's the base of the main vertical power current, and you can imagine it projecting below your torso and between your legs. This chakra is classically associated with "foundational," or survival issues. While any problems you may have in this chakra can manifest that way, the root chakra's most important function is grounding your energy field to the Earth. When that's disrupted, it's likely you'll feel as though you don't belong here and that your existence has no purpose.

Chakra 2: Sacral Chakra
This chakra is part of the spiritual energy system for the sexual organs in both men and women. It's the first chakra that appears on the front and back, and a disruption here can affect our self-identity and ability to relate to other people.

Chakra 3: Solar Plexus Chakra
This chakra exists at the same point as the solar plexus in your nervous system, which is two to three inches below the notch at the center of your ribs and just in front of your spine. The primary function for this chakra is to express your *Will*. Your Will is the energy that puts your choices into action, and I have more information about the Will in an upcoming section.

Chakra 4: Heart Chakra
This chakra is located at the level of your physical heart, but in the center of your chest instead of off to the left. Traditionally, the heart chakra is related to love but it's more than that to me. In addition to love, your heart chakra can help direct your life in profound ways. The phrase "follow your heart" means becoming aware of the heart chakra's energy and what it's communicating to your mind and body. The heart chakra also holds your integrity. Following the direction laid out for you by your heart chakra enables you to live an authentic life that is uniquely perfect for you. This naturally leads to the highest order of integrity. If you aren't living at this high level of integrity, then there is a good chance that you have an energy imbalance affecting your heart chakra.

Chakra 5: Throat Chakra

The Throat Chakra is traditionally associated with our ability to communicate, but there is much more to this one as well. In addition to self-expression, the throat chakra has the important function of recognizing truth and being able to express the truth. Having an imbalance at this level can make a person very susceptible to manipulation since their capacity to recognize truth may be affected. And there is, of course, the obvious: anyone who feels compelled to lie has a definite imbalance in this chakra.

Chakra 6: Third Eye Chakra

This chakra is the center of our intuition and imagination. It's located right between the eyebrows. Your imagination and problem-solving skills are at their best when the third eye chakra is fully active. When this chakra is fully active, imagination becomes creation. You have the capacity to see what's possible and imagine how it can be done. An imbalance here frequently leads to thinking something *can't* be done, rather than focusing on *how* it can be done. This chakra is also the center of your insight into things, events, and people. Highly developed insight is called *clairvoyance*. This is the ability to intuit why things are the way they are and how they got that way.

Chakra 7: Crown Chakra

The Crown Chakra projects out the top of your head at the end of your main vertical power current. It's your Human Energy Field's primary connection to spiritual energy. The crown chakra is often associated with wisdom. Becoming disconnected here means that your entire chakra energy system loses its access to spiritual energy and has only the grounding, or Earth energy, to work with. The Earth energy is not enough by itself to allow you to grow spiritually. An imbalance at this level reduces the amount of spiritual energy your field can draw into itself, and your other chakras will most likely be underpowered. This can lead to symptoms that may appear to come from an imbalance in a different chakra. Resolving an issue with the crown chakra may mean you'll need help from someone with deep awareness *plus* the ability to know which other chakras are affected – along with the ability to make the corrections needed.

Chakra 8: Soul Chakra

I've never seen a reference to the eighth chakra in any text, or a description of it either. What I'm sharing here comes solely from my own observation and experience. The soul chakra is a connection, but a different type of connection than the seventh chakra. While the crown chakra is an energy connection, the Soul chakra is an *information* connection. Specifically, the eighth chakra connects the manifested part of your Soul (the part in your body) with the unmanifested part of your Soul (your Higher Self- the part still remaining with the Spirit group). The soul chakra is the link between those two parts, and it's how we can have access to greater and greater levels of awareness. As we grow spiritually, we're able to draw more information from the vast knowledge of our unmanifested Soul and bring it into our consciousness here. This connection is the reason we're able to grow spiritually and why we'll all eventually be able to directly connect with the Evolving Divine Consciousness while we're still in a physical body. There are people on the Earth right now who have this connection, and others have had this connection in the past. The number of Souls being able to make this connection while still in a physical body has increased over the past few decades. In a sense, the soul chakra is what makes spiritual growth possible here on Earth.

There are a number of minor chakras in addition to the eight main chakras. There is a minor chakra in each hand and each foot, plus one in each elbow, knee, shoulder, and hip. Others exist too, but there

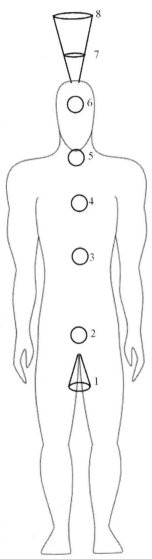

The positions of the chakras: 1)Root chakra; 2)Sacral chakra; 3)Solar plexus chakra; 4)Heart chakra; 5)Throat chakra; 6)Third Eye chakra; 7)Crown chakra; 8)Soul chakra

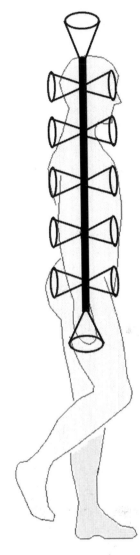

The chakra system from the side. The dark central line is the Main Vertical Power Current. Note that the second through sixth chakras appear on the front and back.

isn't much written about them because their functions come mainly from their connection to the primary chakras and energy system. You can think of them like the outlets in an electrical system – they're essentially receptacles for energy connections that you make with other people and your environment.

The Energy Template

The Energy Template part of your energy field is virtually identical to your physical body, with one important difference: it's like a 3D pencil-line sketch of all the structures in your body with the lines drawn by energy rather than by pencil. All the details are there, even if you "look" down to the cellular level.

The reason the template is important is that any process that disrupts or damages the energy lines ultimately weakens the physical structure. Weakening the structure makes it more susceptible to illness and injury. Therefore, when providing any sort of energy healing, it's wise to be sure the energy template is restored as a part of the process. It's better for the person receiving the healing energy, and they'll most likely get better faster. I know this is beyond the ability of some energy healers currently working, but becoming able to perceive, assess, and correct problems at the energy template level will help your clients to heal more quickly and more completely.

The Astral/Emotional Body

As you've probably guessed, this body is the part of our energy field that exists on the Astral Plane. It's what holds our consciousness during many "out-of-body" experiences and any dreams that occur on the Astral Plane. This body physically looks like us, but its appearance is less sharp – it essentially looks like a fuzzy or blurry version of "us."

This level also houses the *spiritual results* of our physical emotions. Negative emotions can cause negative energy to collect in the Emotional body, and positive energy makes it brighter and more radiant. Energy healers that "pull" out negative energy are generally working at this level. That's often helpful, but there are times when that level isn't "high" enough and healing is needed in higher level bodies like the Causal, Mental, or Soul bodies.

The Causal Body
The Causal body is the part of our energy field that exists on the Causal Plane. This is the level of our energy field that holds our "karma" – the process of correcting the mistakes we've made in the past.

If we've made a real mess of things, this "mess" will show in the Causal Body as different types of energy disruptions. Any energy healer working at this level needs to be careful to leave in place any karmic debt that has not yet been repaid. These debts show as energy disturbances in the Causal field, and the healer must be able to perceive the karmic connections in order to safely work at this level. If the healer attempts any correction of an unpaid karmic debt, two primary things could happen as a result.

The first possibility is that your healing attempt won't work. This is actually a good thing since it leaves the debt in place until it's time to repay it. However, if a healer were to force the correction and succeed, then things in their client's life would have to reorganize in order to repay that debt.

If it's "planned" to be repaid during this specific lifetime and isn't, this will negatively affect a future or upcoming lifetime to make room for that extra burden. The other thing that happens is that the healer will incur a karmic debt themselves that they'll need to repay. All this really means is that energy healing should be gently done. Anything that needs to be forced is better left alone.

The Mental Body

This energy body is the home of our thoughts and imagination. This is the part of our energy field that exists on the Mental and Etheric Planes. Thoughts are strong at this level, and can create forms out of energy. That includes both positive and negative thoughts.

Disruptive or negative thinking creates negative thought forms at this level and causes negative energy to accumulate in the Mental body. Positive thoughts accumulate clear, pure spiritual energy at this level. Now, I'll say up front that controlling our thoughts can be inordinately difficult. They will often arise unbidden, and there doesn't seem to be much we can do to stop them. However, there is something we can do that helps a great deal with this problem.

The source of these unbidden and often negative thoughts is our *ego*. Putting effort into positive spiritual growth often weakens the ego's hold on us, and it's entirely possible *in this lifetime* to grow to the point where our ego becomes so weakened it can no longer take action. That's a state we all can and should strive for. The good news is that the information in this book is a great start on that process, so be sure to read and reread it until the information is fully integrated into your consciousness.

The Soul Body

The Soul Body is the highest level of the Human Energy

Field. It's the part of our Soul that manifests into this space/time universe. The Soul Body is the true essence of each individual. It's the part of us that is Divine and contains a small "spark" of the Evolving Divine Consciousness.

Healing at this level is outside the scope of most energy healers. Imbalances at this level often relate to past life karma, past Spirit group errors that need to be corrected, and imbalances in Soul energy due to serious spiritual infractions. Any energy healing at this level needs a healer who has a deep awareness and is in touch with Soul energy and Spirit groups.

I call the work that I do at this level *Soul energy balancing.* Unfortunately, it may be difficult to find healers who truly work at this level since there are very few. I don't currently know of any other energy healers – other than myself - who do this type of work. I know they exist, but I can't help direct anyone to them because I don't know who they are – at least as of this writing.

One last point on this topic: you may need spiritual help at this level if you've worked with other energy healing practitioners, such as Reiki practitioners, shaman, or energy healers that work directly on the Human Energy Field, and you find they're unable to resolve what you're sure is a spiritual imbalance. If you're in this situation, be sure to meditate and place your need for this level of healing out into the spiritual worlds. If you do this your call will very likely be answered.

Our higher Spiritual Energy System
The manifested part of our Soul, as the foundation of our Human Energy Field, is only a small part of our complete

Soul. The vast majority of our individual Soul (our "Higher Self") resides with our Spirit group, and the Spirit groups exist in the higher spiritual planes of the Universal Spiritual World.

This part of us is beyond knowledgeable and wise. It's directly linked to the Planetary Spirit, and thus the Galactic Spirit and Evolving Divine Consciousness. It's possible to be actively aware of our Higher Self and have a conscious connection to the Evolving Divine Consciousness when we're sufficiently spiritually advanced. This is an important goal for us as spiritual beings. I have had many experiences at this level of consciousness, and I'm personally working toward maintaining this connection permanently during my remaining time here on Earth.

Spiritual principles and spiritual law

I'm fairly sure most people reading this will have at least come across the phrase "spiritual law." I admit that the idea of spiritual laws always seemed logical, but naming them and defining them according to our inherently limited points of view seems a bit illogical to me.

As I've thought about this over time, I've come to realize that there seems to be *only one* true spiritual law, rather than a complex set of "rules" set out for us to follow. I know it will seem a bit minimalist to think about there being just one spiritual law, but I think, once you consider it, you may understand my conclusion. Here is my statement of what I think may be the only spiritual law we have and need:

Choose only thoughts and actions that allow you and Spirit to evolve.

A simple way to do that could be to ask yourself this question any time you have an unclear choice: Which of my choices gives me and others the best opportunity to evolve spiritually? I think starting here will lead to a clearly better choice in almost every circumstance. A second "check" for this could be whether your choice is in accord, or agreement, with what you feel is right in your heart.

Once you understand which choice creates the most spiritual evolvement and your direction is clear, the next step is taking the necessary action. In most cases, I believe honestly answering this question and taking action will align you with the "momentum" of spiritual growth.

A logical question at this point is, "How do you recognize the direction and momentum of spiritual growth?" Although it's logical, it's a bit of a trick question – because we already have the answer. Taking the action that provides the most opportunities for spiritual growth *is* the momentum of spiritual growth. So you're working in alignment with Spirit once you answer that question. One caveat, however… you need to be on the lookout for rationalization – rationalizing a bad choice to make it *look* like the right choice.

Rationalizing a bad choice doesn't change it from a wrong choice to a right choice. Making a wrong choice comes from having limited points of view, like our own egos do, or from limiting thoughts and beliefs we've accepted as true from others – including religions. Having blinders of any sort often leads to decisions that work *against* the current of spiritual growth. Simply take off the blinders, look for the choice that provides the greatest opportunity for growth, and you're sure to be on the right track.

Heart, Will, and Fate

To me, the essences behind heart, will, and fate interrelate. While they do connect in some ways, each does have its own distinct purpose. Here's how I see them interrelate in an ideal world: the heart is the guide, the will is the energy or force behind the guide, and fate is the result. Let's look at each one in a bit more detail, then I'll expand on their relationship after that.

Heart

Heart is something we've all heard of, and we all have some idea of what it means. I'm going to give it a specific meaning for this explanation. To me, *heart* in a spiritual sense is our connection to spiritual guidance. From that, we get our morality – our sense of what is right and wrong. As I see it, that specific moral sense is the *lowest* form of spiritual guidance we receive through our heart. Much more than that is available to us if we're open.

We will forge a more positive path throughout our lives if our heart is genuinely open to guidance from Spirit, and this makes reaching our spiritual goals much easier. True guidance from Spirit has an energy all its own, and it's an energy you've probably felt before. I'd suspect that you, just like me, have felt strongly about doing something specific and let fear (or fear from others) talk you out of doing it – to your regret.

To me, true guiding spiritual energy feels like a "buzzing" energy that lifts my energy, drives my mind into high gear, and has urgency to it – it's something that must be done, and done *now*. It's important to take action right away. I know I've experienced this energy and let fear get in the way. This kept me from taking action and I regretted that later. If you think about, you probably have, too.

I firmly believe that you'll have much less regret in your life if you follow that call from your heart instead of giving in to fear. As you trust that feeling more, and follow its guidance, you'll find it gets easier and easier to ignore the fear and do the right thing. Each step you take while following your heart is a step toward fulfilling your maximum spiritual potential.

The Will

The will is the energy that puts your choices into motion. Because of this, we need to be careful about the driving force behind our will. When we're in full spiritual consciousness, that driver is our spiritual heart, which is in turn being guided by our Higher Self and the Evolving Divine Consciousness. But what else can drive the will? That something else is the *ego*.

The ego is the part of us that, prior to true spiritual awakening, is the driving force behind our will. This is not good news if we want to express a spiritual or divine perspective and act in accord with spiritual principles. When our ego is driving, we put our energy behind what we *want* – but that's not necessarily what's *right*.

I had an experience quite a few years ago at a Spiritualist church. A couple of friends invited me to a service, thinking I'd find it interesting. There was a guest minister who gave a short sermon and then provided some people present with "messages." He provided messages to five or six people, and each time he did he'd point toward the person, tell them, "They have a message for you" and then deliver that message. After these initial five or six messages, he gestured to me and said, "They have a message for you - is that all right?" I thought it was a bit odd that he asked my permission since he didn't with anyone else.

I replied that it was OK, and he did something else he hadn't done with anyone else. He asked a question: "Do you think you're a powerful person?" I inwardly thought yes, but hedged it a bit outwardly and simply said "Somewhat." He then said, "Well, you are. You have a great capacity to channel spiritual energy and tremendous power, but you must remember to direct that power with your heart and not your will."

That wasn't a new concept for me, and I thought I understood it fairly well at that point – but I later realized I was wrong. I had an *intellectual* understanding of what he meant, but I lacked a true spiritual understanding of how important it was to have my spiritual heart in control of my will. In fact, at that time, I thought my spiritual heart *was* in control of my will, but it turns out I was wrong about that too. I also erroneously thought that I had to *give up* my will to be truly spiritual – and that never worked well at all.

I came to realize over time, and with more experience, that my will was simply a force to set things in motion. It genuinely has no volition of its own. I then understood that there were only two drivers for my will – my spiritual heart, acting in accord with spiritual law, or my ego. I suspect that's the case with almost all of us, and most of us, most of the time, have our ego at the controls. How, then, do you put your heart in the driver's seat of your will?

The answer is both simple and, in this world, often difficult to do. The simple answer is to be an open expression of the Evolving Divine Consciousness every moment of your waking life. Yes, that means with all the "stuff" going on in our everyday lives that leaves many of us tired, irritated, frustrated, and feeling that life is a burden. Clearly, being an open expression of the EDC is not a simple thing to do. There are, however, relatively simple things you can do to work *toward* that goal while still managing your daily routine. Here are a few suggestions:

1) Be kind to everyone you meet. It's easy to give in to pressures and irritation, but recognize that everyone you meet is, in consciousness, connected to you. People will generally like you better if you treat them kindly, you'll feel much better about yourself, and you'll most likely have a positive effect on them too. Who knows how much good will come from that? Perhaps a great deal.

2) Be considerate of others feelings, thinking about how you would feel if you were in their place. Before you act or react to something, think about the most likely result of what you're about to do. How will that affect you and others? Is there a better choice you can make right now? If so, do it.

3) Help as many people as you reasonably can each day in small ways without thought of reward.

4) Find a short time for meditation as often as you can. I'll provide a short meditation after this list to get you started.

5) Live your life with integrity and honor. Follow your spiritual heart, and do what you feel is right. If you find that you're uncertain, then make the best choice you can at the time and take action on it. It's spiritually better to take action and be wrong than to let fear keep you from doing what you believe is right.

I firmly believe it's important to have high personal standards and unshakeable integrity. What I've come to realize, however, is that imposing those standards onto others, or having expectations of others, is essentially an attempt to assert my will over someone else's will, or, actually, the divine order Itself. A far better approach is to work from the "assumption" that everyone you meet will do what they've agreed to do, and to flow with every situation as it unfolds. It's OK if the result is different from your plan as long as you're taking positive action. It's quite possible that the different outcome is simply a divine correction to a flaw in your personal plan you may not have perceived.

A beginning meditation

There are numerous resources available to learn about meditation. I firmly believe that the system is less important than your intent, and that you actively practice meditating. The reason it's important is because your true goal should be to *have every moment of your waking life be a form of meditation.*

With this in mind, I'd like to share a very basic meditation just to get you started, if you need it. When you're ready for more help with meditation, there is a website that has excellent study programs that are educational and worth pursuing. You'll find the website address in the Resources section.

Remember, this meditation is for use when you are alone and have some quiet time. It's NOT something you'd want to do while driving or doing anything that needs your focus and attention. Here is the basic meditation:

Take a few slow, deep breaths, and feel your body relax. In your mind, picture a door glowing with soft golden light flowing out from around the edges. Visualize your hand reaching out to the doorknob, grasping it, and pulling the door toward you to open it. The door opens onto an empty room, and you notice a globe of golden-white light just below the ceiling in the center. You notice that golden light is falling like a mist out of the globe, and softly raining down under it. Step forward into the golden mist. Feel the mist envelop you. Feel your body tingling as the light falls on it, and feel your body absorbing this pure energy as it covers you.

Rest here a few minutes, feeling the warmth and purity of this energy. Do not be concerned if you have any other thoughts or feelings; simply let them arise and immediately let them go. When you feel ready, turn around and leave the room by walking through the open door. Close the door behind you and open your eyes.

You can do this any time you want to, whether that's several times per day or once in a while when you think of it. Although you can do fine with just this meditation, I encourage you to explore at least some of the numerous options available in order to make meditation a regular part of your spiritual practice.

Fate

The first thing to mention about fate is that there is no "set" or "predetermined" fate or future. Everything that happens, including things people believe were "meant to be," happens as a result of the choices made by everyone involved in that particular circumstance. In other words, everything that happens is a result of the interaction between *cause* and *effect*.

It should be no surprise that actions have consequences. It should also be clear that the best outcomes result from the most positive choices. In that way, if we each make the most positive and supportive choices we can, we inevitably create a better and more positive future. This, in a spiritual sense, is absolute.

One thing that may come to mind is this: if I make positive choices all the time, will I always get what I want? As much as I'd like to say "yes," the answer is still "no." And there is a good reason.

Other people around you are making choices too, and their collective choices may be pushing events in a different direction. It could be "one against the masses" and momentum favors the masses. So other people's choices could be a reason you don't get something you want.

Another reason is that we sometimes work against *ourselves*. Our conscious mind could be pushing in one direction, and our subconscious mind could be either pushing in a different direction or slamming on the brakes. Since the subconscious mind is the bigger kid, your subconscious mind will win most of the time. The effort you need to put forth, then, is to bring your subconscious mind on board with your conscious mind.

As an example, I can tell you that I've tried many different things within the last 6 or 7 years to create an independent income. I essentially failed at all of them. When I closely examined this problem and looked at my subconscious ideas and inner desires, I knew that everything I was doing was from my conscious mind – but against my subconscious mind and heart.

Ultimately, I had to accept that I would keep failing at anything I tried because I was doing the wrong things. In my heart, I knew exactly what I should be doing: I'm a spiritual teacher. I denied this consciously for years, thinking that no one would care about anything I had to say. I no longer deny the truth since I now have the certainty that it's time to share that knowledge.

The critical message here is this: your heart knows what you need to be doing and what's right for you. Your subconscious mind will be in conflict with your conscious mind until you accept your purpose and unite your heart, mind, and subconscious to all work together. Once you bring all three into alignment, your true journey will begin – even if it begins with small steps.

Each small step is critically important once you're on the right path. If you think about it, every distance, from inches to light-years, is made up of smaller increments that all need to be traveled. What's most important is not the distance, but *being on the right path*. You can't reach your spiritual goals if you're on the wrong path, regardless of how far you travel on that path. Conversely, every single step along the right path brings you closer to realizing your spiritual goals.

Integrity and Truthfulness

Integrity and truthfulness are essential to true, meaningful spiritual growth. Without both of these in place, it's very easy to get lost into the Ego and the illusions it casts to keep itself "in charge" of our consciousness. This is because not having integrity and truthfulness causes us to rationalize our choices, and essentially talk ourselves into believing that our choices – even if they're predominantly negative – are the best choices we can make for our spiritual growth.

However, with the Ego in charge, this is a delusion and a trap. Integrity and truthfulness, with the honesty those require, are essential for keeping the illusions of the Ego at bay and our lives on the true spiritual path we need for growth.

Maintaining integrity and truthfulness in this world is harder than I feel it ought to be. Many people in this world *want* to live in illusion and under delusion. It allows them to be a victim, rather than responsible for their world and what's in it. It's the easy way out, so maintaining your integrity, and being honest and truthful, require greater strength in this world than pretending to be a victim.

Pretending to be a victim is a costly choice to make for someone yearning for spiritual growth and understanding. It undermines your sense of personal responsibility, and this weakens you as a person because you'll believe that responsibility for your well being lies in someone else's hands – often the government. Unfortunately, trying to assume responsibility for everyone and everything weakens our government and weakens our society.

From a spiritual perspective, it's much better to take direct responsibility for your own well-being and spiritual growth. After all, no one cares about your growth more than you do. And, if someone does, that's a sure indicator that you're choosing to believe you're a victim. You can simply choose to *not* be a victim, to take responsibility for your choices, and to start making choices that support your goal of growing your spiritual awareness.

When you make this choice, you'll begin creating a solid, stable foundation for your spirituality – a foundation so strong it cannot be broken by anyone with a more confined point of view. You'll come to possess a level of surety, confidence, and peace that will fill your being with the comfort of knowing, beyond any doubt, that you are on your true spiritual path.

Religion

Religious "faith" is mainly for people who are not yet truly spiritual aware, or who choose to remain spiritually unaware. True faith has nothing to do with the corrupt religious organizations we have created in our society. Religious organizations exist mainly for people who are unaware of the true nature of spirituality.

The intensity of some people's feelings about their religion can be misleading to people on a search for spiritual truth. Strong belief in ideas – even if those ideas are wrong – gives the believer a tremendous amount of conviction. With that conviction comes sincerity and power. Unfortunately, that conviction also lends a great deal of *verisimilitude:* the *appearance* of truth. Often, however, real truth is lacking.

True faith has nothing to do with religion, and true faith has no need *for* religion. When a person has true faith, they understand that their existence is purposeful, and that God (the creator and Evolving Divine Consciousness), is incomplete without them. They know their understanding will grow as they become more attuned to and aligned with the consciousness that created our universe.

This is the understanding that comes from true faith: that every single one of us is a part of the Spirit that is the foundation of all consciousness, and we are coming to know and understand more of the nature and purpose of this Spirit, or God. Think about this: would anyone with that level of understanding need the limiting precepts of an organized religion? It's clear to see they would not.

There is something else I'd like to say about religion,

knowing full well that some folks reading this next thought will have a strong, knee-jerk reaction to it – but you need to understand it: Religion is one of the most destructive forces in this world.

I say this for a very specific reason. It's responsible for more wars and death than any other reason any war has been fought over. However, it also serves a very specific spiritual purpose: To keep us from gaining deep spiritual knowledge before we're ready for it. That means we're destined to have wars and religion until nearly all of this world's inhabitants have graduated from spiritual kindergarten. Once that happens, then this world will eventually be ready to live without religion and without wars.

Now you may be wondering: What does "ready for" deep spiritual knowledge mean? Simply evolving spiritually to the point where almost everyone on this planet can clearly see and understand that conventional religions pass along *some* spiritual truths, but wrap those simple truths in too much dogma and interpretation. You don't need anyone to tell you "What Jesus meant by that was...."

Once you're open to learning a deeper spiritual understanding, you'll have a personal understanding of spiritual truth. You'll come to realize you *don't* need an intermediary. You'll come to realize that the road to spiritual mastery is there for you, too, and you'll come to realize you walk that path with all others *as equals*.

This is something most religious leaders mislead themselves and other people about. They often think of themselves as intermediaries, or God's "vehicle" to help you here on Earth. Truth is, you never need to sit and listen to anything that begins with "What Jesus meant was..." or

68

"What God wants is…." Any answer to either of those statements can't be anything more than someone else's interpretation or opinion – what they think or believe the answer to be.

Now tell me: if you honestly believe that they're best qualified to answer spiritual questions for *everyone* just because they went to school and got hand-fed other people's ideas, then you go ahead and sit and listen. If that's you, then you're not ready to move on to deeper spiritual truths, and it's best for you to stay where you are until you truly know it's time to move forward. If that's not you, then you're ready to know that no one standing at any pulpit has any right to tell you what Jesus *meant* – he *said* what he meant, so simply think about what those words mean and what you can learn from them.

And, in my opinion, anyone who attempts to tell someone else "What God wants…" is not worth listening to. In their case, it will only be what the religious leaders want you to know, and not at all what *you* need to know. So, when thinking about what God wants for you, the only authority worth listening to is *you.*

I have one more point to make here, but I won't be able to explain it fully until I discuss Spirit evolving in a couple of chapters The point I want to make is this: The "religion" taught through most religious organizations is designed to feed into and communicate with our Ego, and not our Spirit. Basically, anyone who tells us we need to be "God-fearing," or that we're sinners, or too small to be spiritually strong on our own, is either seriously misleading you or outright lying to you.

Thinking that we're sinners, or need to fear God, or anything similar, are things that feed our Ego and keep it from trying to grow and evolve – which it can't do. Those things also help our egos to avoid change. Egos like that because egos hate change, and want things to stay the way they are. So basically, if you're not ready to embrace change, you're not ready for true spiritual growth.

Direct evidence of religion's actual functions is easy to spot when you know what to look for. It's right up front, in the form of contradictions. Things like, "God is Love" and "God-fearing" can't really coexist. But, by offering up both in the same breath, religions string people along by offering them hope – "God is Love" – while at the same time keeping them down and under their control. I'll bet we've all heard others extolling someone else's Christian virtues by referring to them as God-fearing.

Just for the record, there is no need to *ever* fear God. God is not punitive, and will not punish you or anyone else in any way. Bad things that happen in people's lives happen because of *choices* – choices that both they and other people make. It's also important to know that God is so much more than love, and does **not** have a pre-designed plan for each of us.

Believing God is love genuinely limits God, and we place this limit to try and fit the concept of God into our human understanding. As our creator, God is far more than everything we can think, feel, or imagine. I feel our best relationship with God is to view our creator as a beacon – a beacon drawing us forward into our full potential.

As you may now see, a true seeker of spiritual knowledge cannot remain confined to a single religious point of view and hope to reach meaningful enlightenment. Having enlightenment as a spiritual goal means you'll need knowledge that comes from a spectrum of today's religions, along with the experience that comes from personal spiritual exploration.

Prayer

I believe that many people cling to religion in part because of a misguided perception: that only those who are religious have the "right" to pray. I want to correct that misperception and tell you that we all have every right to pray. But, if we're not "religious," then who will we pray to?

It turns out that, religious or not, prayer always goes to the same place first. When we pray, our prayers ascend to our Soul in our Spirit group. From there, our Soul sends out the request into the Universal Spiritual World. Then, if it's spiritually correct to do so, an angel or other spiritual being will respond to help.

From that perspective, it's easy to see that prayer does not belong to religions. It's simply a way for us to communicate with our Soul and get spiritual help from others. If you regularly pray, there is no need for you to give up something important to you - even if you're ready to move past the confines of conventional religions.

Negative emotions and negative events

Something I've wondered is, "Why do we have negative emotions?" They most often seem to only hurt us and others; any good that comes from them generally comes later, when we return to a more positive or calm state of mind. So what are they for? And how can we change them if we have them?

I believe negative emotions are nothing more than coping mechanisms for the ego. Without having the ego "in charge" of our daily lives, we genuinely have no need for negative emotions. Let's look at a couple of examples to examine this.

I'd like to briefly explore *irritation* and *frustration*. What's happening when we experience these emotions? To me, we have these emotions when *the world doesn't conform to how we want it to be.* We get upset when someone else does something we don't like. We get irritated at people for behaving in ways we don't like. We get frustrated when things don't work the way we want them to. The one constant among all these things is clearly the notion that what we *think* things should be like is what the whole world *should* be like. The question is, then: Why do we think our way is the right way?

It's relatively simple: we're comfortable with our way. We know what to do, how to act, and what's going to happen if we follow our own internal rules. For many people, mostly those with less experienced souls, this greatly reduces the unknown and that in turn reduces fear and discomfort. As we learn and grow, it becomes painfully apparent that none of us controls everything, and that things we don't like happen despite our attempts at control.

Anger

Anger, by itself, is neither positive nor negative. By itself, being angry can be a justified emotion. Or it can also be misplaced. If it is justified and leads you to take positive, corrective action, then your anger made a positive difference. On the other hand, misplaced anger often becomes a cancer in a person's soul. It can cause a person to blame others for things that are actually their own fault. This is a highly distorted perspective that often leads to self-loathing, misdirected hate, and many other negative emotions.

I believe anger is often misunderstood in a spiritual context. Most people believe that someone who experiences anger can't be truly spiritual. I believe this is a fallacy. Anger is a natural emotion, and can be applied to make positive changes. It can also provide the determination to take heroic measures to protect those we love. From a spiritual perspective, this is a positive use of anger.

If anger is something you regularly experience, look deeply at the cause. If it's amplified irritation at things you simply don't like, then that is a spiritual problem you'll need to address. If it's directed toward genuine injustices and it spurs you to take action, then it's a positive force you can harness and use to benefit yourself and others.

Worry

Worry, simply put, is an absolute waste of mental and spiritual energy. Before we get too far into worry, I want to differentiate *worry* from *concern*. The difference is simple: Worry is about things that *could* or *may* happen. *Concern* is about things that *are* happening.

That's an important distinction. It's natural, understandable, and emotionally healthy to be concerned about things that are actually happening. What's not emotionally healthy is being worried about all the things that *may* happen. Being worried about all the "What if's" you can dream up is an absolute waste of mental and spiritual energy. You must recognize that *worrying about "what if's" is wasted energy because close to none of the "what if's" ever happen.*

If you find yourself worrying, assert some mental discipline and be determined to only be concerned about what *is* and to not worry about what *if*. It's a choice you can make, and it's something only you can change if it's a problem for you. The point is *you can change it* if you choose to.

Anxiety

I believe worry and anxiety are relatively modern emotions. When a group is busy with daily survival, they put their energy into dealing with whatever comes their way. There's not much energy left for creating an unimportant list of "what if's?" This means that these two emotions only come into play *when our very survival is not threatened daily.*

This is an important point. If these emotions only arise once basic survival is reasonably assured, then what useful purpose can worry and anxiety serve? The answer is clear to me: *none.*

Anxiety comes, at least in my opinion, from a lack of self-esteem. When anxiety keeps people from doing things, they'll often say they "can't." What they really mean is, "I don't want to because I'm afraid of what might happen." That's very different from *can't*. I physically can't jump across a 20-foot wide chasm. I know what will happen if I try. I'm not afraid of what *might* happen; I already know what *will* happen.

On the other hand, I'm a bit uncomfortable walking up to a complete stranger in public to ask them a question if I need help. I don't *want* to do it, but I know there are times I may *need* to do it, and I won't let my discomfort control my actions. Any anxiety over doing this is less important to me than my desire to not let limiting emotions control my behavior.

I think anxiety is, in some sense, an opposite of self-confidence. Someone with self-confidence generally has the determination to assert their self-control and not let anxiety dictate their actions. With self-confidence, a person knows they have the capability to manage any situation AND the ability to accept any and all consequences.

Something I'd like to bring up that sometimes comes into play with extreme anxiety is a panic attack. Since the symptoms of a panic attack closely mirror those of a heart attack, I think there are a certain percentage of panic attacks that are physically based. Anyone that has a panic attack should rule out a physical heart condition to be on the safe side. On occasion, medication may also be necessary to help manage panic attacks while the person is working on other ways to control the attacks.

But what if your emotions stop you from doing things, or your choices leave you unsure about what to do? That happens to everyone, but if it's a consistent problem in your life there are ways you can get over it.

Taking action regardless of your emotions

Most people's emotions influence their actions – or keep them from taking action – far more frequently than necessary. The plain and simple truth is that our actions, barring outside control, are our choice. We, and only we, decide what we will do.

I'm sure many reading this will think it's not that simple, or that statement really doesn't apply to them, or I'm just plain wrong. The actual truth is that any thought that contradicts this simple truth is a rationalization. Your conscious mind is in control of your actions, and your emotions should NOT be.

It's easy to get into the grip of our emotions and declare them responsible for our actions. It's simple, but it abdicates our conscious responsibility. It's also a choice, and a poor one at that. Instead, we can easily learn to take the right actions *regardless* of what our emotions are saying. We don't need to be compelled to action by *any* of our emotions. That includes rage, passion, fear, love, and any other emotion you can name. You're never the victim of your emotions, even if you don't know that to be true. It is true regardless of your belief.

The process of taking action despite your emotions is deceptively simple, and it has nothing to do with *why* you're feeling the emotions, *what* emotions you're feeling, or the root cause behind those particular emotions in the first place. ***None of that matters.***

Trying to get to the root of why you're having emotions, hoping that will lead to some understanding and the possibility that you may eventually overcome those emotions is a foolish waste of time. You have the emotions; where they came from is irrelevant. What *isn't* irrelevant is what you do with them, and how you respond to them. That's all that matters. The rest is wasted effort that can at best inch you toward a shaky chance of success. Make the choice to stop wasting your time, and follow the steps I'm about to lay out for you.

The essence of not being a slave to your emotions is this: feel them, and take the right action regardless of what your emotions are "compelling" you to do. You may have heard this phrased as, "Feel the fear and do it anyway." This holds true for *any* emotion, not just fear. So – how can you do that? How do you feel an emotion that you believe is compelling you to take a specific action (or, conversely, to not take action) without following that emotion, and how do you do something else entirely?

The secret lies in learning how to feel your emotions without them affecting the inner "you." Accomplishing this is simpler than it may seem, and, if you do it, it's guaranteed to work.

The simplest and fastest way to accomplish this is to do everything you don't like to do or have been putting off FIRST and IMMEDIATELY. By doing this, you're training your mind to take immediate action despite whatever your emotions may be. A natural side benefit is that you're getting things done that would normally cause you to procrastinate. Be sure to start with the tasks that cause the most procrastination, and work down your "don't want to do" list before you even think about your "like to do list."

Several things will happen when you do this. As mentioned, you'll be getting all those distasteful things done. But more importantly, you'll still be feeling your emotions when you're doing them, and you'll be training yourself to take action regardless of how you feel. What will happen over time is that the emotions holding you back will start to lose their energy. They're not being fed; they're being starved. Those emotions will get weaker and less insistent, and even easier to ignore. In time, you'll be able to feel *any* emotion without it dictating your actions.

As a quick side note, it's important that the things on your list – whether they're things you do or don't want to do, need to be in accord with spiritual law. Anything *not* in accord with spiritual law doesn't belong on *any* to-do list.

Notice that you will not be putting any energy into trying to *control* your emotions. I believe that's essentially pointless. You're going to feel what you're going to feel. Accept that, and accept that you can systematically weaken the hold that your emotions currently have on you.

You're learning to control your actions, instead of futilely trying to control your emotions. In time, it won't matter whether you feel them or not, and those "blasts" of emotion will fade to twinges that you can very easily ignore. Simply get in the habit of doing what needs to be done regardless of the emotions involved, and you will succeed.

Being offended
"I'm offended" are two dangerous and destructive words. Because of those two little words, many people are now afraid to say what they really think, feel, or believe. Society has allowed those words to create laws that make no sense. Society has also allowed those two words to censure brilliance and to keep challenging, growth-enabling concepts out of the minds of those who could benefit from

those concepts. All because someone else "didn't like it."

Although anyone and everyone has the right to feel as though they're offended, they *don't* have the right to project that onto *anyone* else – and here's why: Feeling offended is a personal **choice.**

Think about this for a moment. No matter what it is under the sun, you can probably find someone who feels offended by it. But you can just as easily find someone else who's *not* offended by it. So... which one is right? Well, they both are within their personal preferences. But neither one is absolutely right, because, in this case, *there is no absolute right. There is only personal opinion and belief.*

Let's pick an example that looks easy: pornography. Many people find pornography offensive. But many people genuinely enjoy it. Now, I know the "offended" group want to make up something about it being a deviant practice, and that the enjoyment stems from some deep-rooted psychological imbalance, etc. And there will be some times that is in fact true.

But, in many other cases, that's just a rationalization imposed by a group of small-minded people who believe that anyone who thinks differently must be "evil," "disturbed," or "off" in some way. Why can't they just be folks who think differently, but are still decent people? Why does it have to be *wrong* to enjoy pornography? The simple answer is that it isn't wrong – it's simply their preference.

I'm not saying that the person who feels offended is under obligation to give up that feeling – they're not. It's their right to feel offended. They need to accept that pornography may not be right for them, but others have the right to enjoy it if they choose. They need to recognize that they *chose* a limiting belief, and others are free to not live under that limitation.

I've found that the teachings of conventional religions generally push people to project their own limiting thought patterns onto other people under the guise of "saving" them. In my opinion, that's invasive and controlling. But since that's my opinion, I really don't care if anyone else takes offense at that. It's your choice – you can keep your thinking small, or you can expand your thinking to grasp the lesson I'm conveying. In that case, you won't be offended.

Being wrong

Being wrong happens to everyone. Every single person on the planet has *some* limitations in their thoughts and perceptions. By itself, being wrong is not negative. Someone who embraces being wrong as an opportunity to learn will learn much faster than someone who is afraid to be wrong and takes no action as a result.

In a similar vein, it's often better to make a "wrong" decision than it is to be afraid and make *no* decision. A "wrong" decision at a minimum leads to a learning opportunity, and sometimes even leads to success. Being paralyzed by fear, however, leads nowhere, and often gets worse as time passes. It's debilitating, and gets to be a bigger problem unless you confront it directly and learn to feel the fear but take action anyway.

If you summon the mental discipline to take action despite your fears, at a minimum your fears will no longer control your life. But I suspect that, over time, you'll understand that those fears are predominantly baseless and they'll probably weaken, or possibly disappear altogether.

Violence

Violence is a part of this world. Bad people exist and do bad things. I want all my readers to know that defending yourself and protecting those you love from harm is NOT against any spiritual law. You can, in good conscience, protect yourself and others from harm.

With that said, it's necessary to also provide some context. To me, and according to the law in most places, there is only one circumstance in which true violence is justified: being in genuine fear for your life or of grave bodily harm – either personally or for a loved one. Violence is simply not necessary under any other circumstances.

This means that other people's words should not anger you and lead to violence. Simple disagreements never need to end in violence. Potential "bar fights" or anything similar can most often be avoided by not responding and by leaving. Don't let anyone else control your actions or provoke you, and reserve violence for the truly rare instances you may need to fight for your life.

And, just to mention it again – it is spiritually permissible for you to protect your life. If you're in that situation, it's because someone else put you in that position. It's *their* actions that have brought things to that point, so the responsibility for the violence – and for the consequences of that violence – belongs to the person who created the situation in the first place.

That brings us to *preparedness*. In this world *meek* often translates into *prey*. Learning to properly protect yourself creates a visible level of confidence that could make you an undesirable target for many predators. That visible level of confidence most often comes from experience or proper training. However, sport-type martial arts probably isn't the training that will serve you best. The only time you'll need violence is to fight for your life. Sport training is not what you need at that moment – you need to learn how to immediately stop a life-threatening predator.

My preference for this type of training is Target Focus Training. Their methods are straightforward, easy to learn, and can save your life. Their website is listed in the Resources section.

Why bad things happen to good people

In addition to violence, we've all had bad things happen to us, to our families, and to people we know. During bad times, many people wonder how God could allow bad things to happen. There is an answer for that, but the answer doesn't actually involve God.

Our universe operates under *free will*. This means we get to choose what we do. This also means that, contrary to some religious beliefs, there is no specific plan laid out for us. There are guidelines, to be sure, but each of us gets to choose our actions – even actions that go against the guidelines.

What that means is this: bad things happen because of the choices made by us *and/or* everyone around us. This means bad things can still happen to us even if we've made the best choices we can. Here is a small example:

I lived in New York, and I was going to college during the day and working in the evening. My school and work were in Nassau County, and I lived with my parents in the

Bronx. One particular night, a co-worker asked if I could give him a ride home and I agreed.

I dropped him off at his home, and got home to park my car about a half hour later than I normally would have. I got out of my car and was approached by three men. One of them walked up to me and said, "Excuse me sir, but this is a good, old-fashioned American stickup." I admit I thought that was clever, and I chuckled in response.

I told him I didn't have much money – all I had in my wallet was a dollar. That obviously wasn't enough for them, so the "spokescrook" asked if I had an ATM card, and I didn't – so they decided to steal my car. I told them I wasn't going to let them have my car, and one of them pulled out a gun. I changed my mind and told them to take the car.

They started to get in the car, then decided to take me with them and forced me into the back seat. We spent a few hours riding around, and there is a bit more to the story, but at the end they took me to a wooded area at the border of the Bronx and Westchester County. They told me to get out, and I thought they were going to shoot me. One of them told me, "Get home safe – you gotta walk through a bad neighborhood." I walked away, waiting for the shot in my back. But I heard the car door close and heard them drive away. I didn't get shot, and I eventually did get home.

As things go, this was an unpleasant experience and, in my opinion, counts as a "bad thing" happening to a good person. But the simple truth is that I made a choice. If I had gone home without the side trip from dropping off my co-worker, it's very likely that those criminals would have been somewhere else. My car may have been stolen – that's still possible – but I most likely wouldn't have been carjacked and kidnapped. A different choice would most likely have had a different outcome.

I do wonder, though, how that affected my spiritual path. Did that "bad" event lead me to greater spiritual growth than I would have had without the bad event? Or did it slow down my spiritual progress? Did it balance a karmic debt? It's very difficult to say what would be different since I have no idea what would have happened had that not taken place. It seems to boil down to this: I made a specific and seemingly small choice that probably changed the direction of my life.

Is it better or worse? Well, that's up to me. Regardless of which way things turn out, as an aware spiritual being I have a responsibility to make the best choices I can, However, I can only make those choices based on what I know at the time. Others make their choices too, and things are set in motion based on those choices. Regardless of the outcome, accepting the result with grace and moving forward is spiritually your best choice.

Good and Evil

We can all see that violence happens and that bad people exist. We can also see that good people exist. That brings up two good questions: 1) Why are there bad people, and 2) How does this fit in with spiritual growth? Let's take a look at the answers.

Bad people exist for the same reason as bad things happen: free will allows us to make choices that hurt others, whether unknowingly or deliberately. But why do we need bad people and bad events as a part of our spiritual growth? The answer is that bad people, bad events, and adversity all make it possible to grow spiritually at a much faster pace.

Think about this for a moment: If we lived in a perfect world of happiness, sunshine, rainbows, and chocolate (personal indulgence there), what could possibly happen that would challenge our perspective? Most likely nothing. We'd be content to be as we are, and there would be no impetus for change and growth. Negative people and negative events give us reasons to want *change*. Think of it this way: almost every great invention of mankind was an answer to a problem.

Without a problem, there is no need for a solution. Without a need for a solution, there is no need to change. Without the need for change - well, nothing ever changes. If nothing changes, we don't have the opportunity to grow spiritually. So, in a sense, bad people, negative events, and adversity are all *required* for spiritual growth here on Earth.

Greed

Greed is one of the most pervasive and fatal cancers in our society. It's responsible for an enormous amount of grief and heartache, violence, poverty, and despair. However, greed itself is misunderstood. Most people think "greed" mainly applies to money. That seems so on the surface. Many people equate "rich" with "greedy."

There are greedy people in every stratum of society. Many people think of rich people as greedy, but "rich" and "greedy" are not the same - there are rich people who are not greedy, and there are many poor people who are. Greed is an inner condition driven by fear, and it's a condition that equates "more" with "better," or "more valuable." Truthfully, "better" and "value" have nothing to do with "more" or greed.

In fact, wealth without greed is what we need to heal our society. It's about the only way we can solve our many problems – and no, those solutions cannot come from a corrupt, bloated government that is the cause of many of these ills and an enormous burden on the American people.

Having a sense of personal, internal worth or value as a person develops internal conditions that can't coexist with greed. An internal sense of worth, or value, comes from the understanding that value is inherent and not driven by the quantity of external things in one's possession.

If you're greedy, there is never "enough." The greedy lack an inner mechanism for self-satisfaction. We've all heard the thinking: "Things will be better once I have...." Rarely is that true. "Things" only get better by changing your thoughts and beliefs, which leads to changing behaviors and making more positive choices.

This is the reason eliminating greed is an important step in repairing our society and will benefit *all* of mankind. The ability to make objective decisions and wise choices can only come from an individual who has learned a true spiritual perspective and outgrown a need for greed.

Just to be clear - I'm not at all saying you can't want to be wealthy. Being wealthy is just fine. Being wealthy gives you options you wouldn't otherwise have. It can also be of substantial help in fulfilling your highest calling or aspirations. All of those things take resources. The more resources you have of your own, the less you'll need to depend on the resources of others to realize your dreams.

You may be wondering how eliminating greed can move humanity onto a better path. Or why that's the first negative human emotion to eliminate.

History has shown us that greed has led to slavery, population control, loss of liberties, wars, famine, and a host of other negative things. Relentless greed leads to rationalizing negative actions and choices by making them seem, at least to the greedy mind, to be in the best interest of everyone. But this is a fallacy. A mind consumed by greed cannot think clearly or be fully rational. It's too busy subconsciously working on ways to benefit itself by accumulating "more."

Those rationalizations lead to believing that taking advantage of others is really in their best interest; after all, where would they be otherwise? This is the subconscious inner dialogue we'd likely hear: "Where would they be without me looking out for them? How could they survive if left on their own? They don't have any way to help themselves, so they're depending on me to help them. And so what if I get rich off their labors? At least they'll have food to eat and a place to stay." And that's the basic process that the greedy will follow to justify their ends and means.

All the while, the inner drive for "more" remains hidden. That inner drive is often rooted in fear - fear that the world won't provide enough; fear that someone could take everything away at any moment; fear that without "more," others will treat them as though they have no value as a person.

That last statement contains the means of defeating greed. Feeling a sense of internal value or self-worth allows a person to move past the need for greed. It eliminates the driving need to fill the void left by having no feeling of inherent worth. Having a sense of inner self-worth is essential to developing inner calmness and strength. It's within that calmness and strength that we make our most positive choices.

Inner calmness and inner strength are essential to developing our full potential so we can help others do the same. In this way, we can, one person and one step at a time, move past the limitations we collectively have and form a new, healthful, and strong society based on personal growth.

How, then, do we develop this inner calmness and inner strength? It starts with a pause. Instead of having instant and knee-jerk reactions to the people and events around us, pause for just a moment before responding. In that moment, consider the most likely possibilities. Consider the outcomes of your actions - good and bad. Ponder ways to eliminate the negative outcomes. Consider how your actions will affect not just you - but those around you too.

And even how their reactions could affect others.

This may seem like a lot to fit into a moment, and it is. But that moment will grow shorter as your mind grows accustomed to thinking in this way. You'll be training your mind to think this way at a subconscious level, so you'll find that, in time, you'll begin to understand the deeper and deeper ramifications of your actions. Your choices will improve. You'll become much better at making choices that benefit not just you, but everyone around you.

Our society will gradually be collectively making better choices as more and more people learn this method of thinking. Negative elements will fit in less and less, and have fewer and fewer proponents. In this way, our society will slowly outgrow the need for greed.

Wealthy visionaries without greed will be critical to saving our country, so it's perfectly OK if you want to be one. Their primary contribution will be in helping others overcome the entitlement mentality, and helping people learn to appreciate the benefits of being financially self-reliant and not a slave to greedy politicians. They'll help restore self-esteem to the American people, and help restore the values of our Founding Fathers – our rights to freedom, independence, and self-reliance.

Health

Physical health is important to spiritual growth. Most of us lead busy lives, and things are simply easier if you're fit. Managing to do everything you need to do in our modern lifestyle – especially if you have a family – takes substantial energy. If you add things to that – like time for meditation and spiritual study – you're taking time from something else, and that can cause stress. You don't need more stress, but you *can* manage to fit more into your day if you're in better condition, compared to if you're not.

This has been an ongoing issue for me. I don't enjoy exercise, but I do enjoy being able to do what I want to do, and feel better doing it. Sometimes I manage to exercise for a few months, then I'm off the wagon again for a little while. I know this has been a weakness, and I'm working toward a different approach – a lifestyle change that will require more physical work. I think this may help since exercise seems like lost time to me, but doing physical work makes me feel as though I'm accomplishing something useful. I know this is a weakness in my perspective, and I'm hoping that this change makes a positive difference.

If getting into shape and being fit is fairly easy for you, you'll have a "leg-up," so to speak, since you'll be able to accomplish more and include spiritual study and meditation. However, there is more to your health than being fit, and a few critical factors I want to briefly mention are the food you eat, your personal environment, personal lifestyle choices, and allergies.

Before I get into those, I'd want to mention a bit about genetics. First, your genetics are what they are. Each person is a genetic blend, and each combination has its own strengths and weaknesses. Although you can't change your genetics, it's best to understand what challenges you may have because of those genetics and to make choices that help to minimize your weaknesses. Now let's get into the importance of the food you eat.

Food makes a difference

What you eat directly affects your body. Any food that is not wholesome has some sort of negative affect on your body, even though you may not be aware of it. Food that isn't heavily processed has more nutrients. Fresh foods without pesticides are a more healthful choice as well.

After all, it's not difficult to see that a poison designed to kill bugs can cause you some harm, even if you're much bigger than a bug. If you're not sure about this, pick up a can of bug spray and check out the label next time you're at the store. Read the warnings, and then think to yourself, "Would I really want to spray this on my food then eat it?" I'll bet the answer will be no.

The best way to avoid pesticides is to grow your own fruits and vegetables. The next best way is to buy organic. It's best to buy as much organic food as you can afford, but some foods generally have more pesticides than others, and buying those organically grown really is your best, most healthful choice. You may have heard of the "dirty dozen" – the fruits and vegetables that tend to have the highest pesticide levels. Buy these organically if at all possible. There is another list called the "clean fifteen," and these are less important to purchase organically. Here are those lists, in case you haven't seen them before:

Dirty Dozen	Clean Fifteen
Apples	Asparagus
Celery	Avocados
Cherry tomatoes	Cabbage
Cucumbers	Cantaloupe
Grapes	Sweet corn
Hot peppers	Eggplant
Kale/ Collard greens	Grapefruit
Nectarines(imported)	Kiwi
Peaches	Mango
Potatoes	Mushrooms
Spinach	Onions
Strawberries	Papayas
	Pineapple
	Sweet peas
	Sweet potatoes

This list may change from time to time as farming practices and regulations change, but it will help you purchase cleaner food and reduce the amount of pesticides you're eating.

Remember that food is more than fuel – it's also what your body is made from. Dirty, poisoned food leaves poisons in your body. It should be fairly obvious that a body with accumulated poisons and toxins cannot be as healthful as a clean and properly nourished body. Eating cleaner food will go a long way toward improving your overall health, and is very likely to help you feel better in the long run. Less illness is less suffering, and you'll probably agree that's a good thing. I know it is to me.

Beverage choices

Plain water is unequivocally your best beverage choice. I'll cover a simple, basic way you can have clean, healthful drinking water at home without the environmental pollution created by billions of empty plastic water bottles. First, I want to focus on three specific things: carbonated drinks, sugary drinks, and coffee.

Carbonated drinks

Carbonated drinks are a horrendous choice of beverage. They're widely consumed, but that doesn't make them a healthful choice. The carbonation isn't good for you, and neither are any of the sweeteners – whether it's high fructose corn syrup, aspartame, or any other artificial sweetener. I know the manufacturers of these sweeteners claim they're safe, but that doesn't mean it's a good idea to put them in your body. I personally believe these drinks are even more harmful to children, even though many foolish people give them to their children regularly. Your health, and your family's health, will benefit if you stop drinking these unnecessary and useless beverages.

Sugary drinks

Artificially colored and sweetened drinks are also a poor choice for you and for your children. Not only is excess sugar bad for you and your children, the artificial colorings and flavorings make them even worse. Excess sugar is the main culprit in our society's high cholesterol problem, and exchanging fats for sugars in "lite" versions of foods just makes the problem even worse. This trend is simply driving more people onto prescribed medications, and that's what the drug companies want. Better health and better living both come from nature and not a chemical factory.

Coffee

I have never been a coffee drinker. I find it interesting that so many people feel they need a stimulant before they can manage their day. I personally believe most coffee drinkers would do just fine without it once they got out of the habit of drinking it and no longer believed they "need" it just to get by. What makes coffee even worse, though, is adding excess sweeteners, whether natural or artificial, and adding chemical flavors. If you're a regular coffee drinker, and especially if you're a frequent coffee drinker, you'd benefit a great deal by eliminating it from your daily routine.

Water

Pure, clean water is your best, most healthful choice of beverage. Pure water is virtually impossible to get, but you can make great drinking water at home fairly easily and inexpensively. The EPA's list of "allowable" contaminants and pollutants for tap water reads like both a nightmare and a chemist's storeroom. Fortunately, there is a simple home solution that solves this problem.

Let's cover tap water first. Many people drink it, most people cook directly with it, and most also bathe or shower in it daily. These may all be safe things to do in some parts of the country, but certainly not in all. Most municipal water is decontaminated by chlorine based products. While they're not good to drink, they're downright toxic to inhale – and most of us do it every day.

Heating water drives off most of the chlorine-based decontaminators, but those chemicals then become vapor that you inhale. Long-term exposure to inhaling them is even worse for your body than drinking them. Because of this, you may want to investigate bath and shower filters that eliminate most of these chlorine-based chemicals so they're no longer forced into the air you breathe when you bathe or shower. For cooking, a simple carbon filter can substantially reduce most of the chlorine compounds so you're not driving them into the air in your home when you cook. In addition, your food is likely to taste better too.

94

Drinking water takes a bit more work, but it's still fairly easy to get very clean drinking water with only a few minute's work each day and without a huge expense. My preference is to use a combination of two things: a carbon-based filter and a countertop distiller. I simply filter the water first to substantially reduce the chlorination, then distill it to remove the other chemical and mineral impurities. The end result is very clean, and very healthful, drinking water. You can use a countertop pitcher or a faucet-mounted filter for filtering. Either is fine, as long as you filter the water *before* distilling it.

Your personal environment

Your living environment may be affecting you more than you realize. Our living environment is actually any place that we physically are, but the places we spend the most time generally have the greatest affect on our health – short of being directly exposed to toxic chemicals or poisons.

The places most of us tend to be most of the time are our home, at work, in our cars, and any other establishments we go to regularly – stores, restaurants, cafes, bars, friend's homes, etc. Toxins or allergens in any of these places can negatively affect your health. It would be almost impossible to know what toxins are present in places we don't control, so it's especially important to control what you can.

At home, you probably have a variety of cleaning supplies that have fragrances and/or warnings on the label. Most chemical cleaners are toxic, and you're spraying those chemicals into the air you breathe every time you use them. It's wise to consider using natural alternatives so you expose your body to fewer toxins. Candles and chemical odor-maskers add significantly to the chemical pollution in homes, so eliminating them would be wise too.

Limiting these things at work could be more problematic, unless you're the company owner and choose to make some positive changes. Since you may not be able to control these things, and since you can't control your coworkers (unless you all come to an agreement), you should at least consider keeping your personal space at work (if you have one) as clear as possible of these common toxins. If you can't even do this, then be on the lookout for any careless handling of chemical toxins that can be a health hazard. Clean up or report any hazards you find.

Your personal care products are important too. Most labels for personal care products read like a chemical catalog, and almost everything in there is to make the product easier to produce and last longer on the shelf. Those chemicals are NOT there to make the product better or safer for you; they're there purely to benefit the company. Simple, natural soaps – preferably castile soaps, made from vegetable ingredients – are your best choice. These soaps generally (but not always) have no harsh chemicals so you won't have those harmful chemicals being absorbed through your skin.

You even have the option of making your own soap and perhaps even some of your personal care products. Making a good castile soap is less complicated than you would think, and the resulting soap is much better and less expensive than commercial soaps. I've personally made soap, and even lip balm, and found it to be much easier than I thought it would be. If this interests you, there are great websites and books with all the information and supplies you'll need.

Your personal lifestyle choices

What you ingest is really up to you, and that includes choosing to indulge in using alcohol, cigarettes, or illegal drugs. You body simply doesn't need *any* of these things to survive. You don't have to go out drinking or get drunk at home. That's expensive and definitely hurts your body. Choosing to not drink is a personal choice, and you can also ignore any attempts at peer pressure if you don't drink.

If you don't want to hurt your body, then don't drink – regardless of what anyone else may be saying or doing. Peer pressure doesn't really exist. Instead, what you're experiencing is a personal internal pressure that *you're* creating because of worry or anxiety about what others "may" think of you. In truth, the opinion of anyone who is busy getting drunk is absolutely unimportant. Always consider the source, and remember that anyone urging you to hurt yourself doesn't have your best interests at heart.

The same thing is true for smoking or using illegal drugs. There is overwhelming evidence that these are harmful things to do, and my opinion is this: anyone who chooses to smoke or use illegal drugs is a fool. It's a stupid choice, and one that's easily avoided. If the fools around you are "pressuring" you to join in, then they're not your friends – leave immediately. Make a positive choice for yourself instead of following an idiot down a dangerous path.

Making wise decisions about your personal lifestyle is something you can choose to do or choose to ignore. I believe it's best for each of us to do what is spiritually responsible and physically possible for us. Just remember that our actions have consequences, and those consequences ripple out to affect others.

Allergies

Many of us have various allergies, and some of us aren't even aware of them. Allergens can be affecting you in different ways every day without you even being aware of it. Many allergens have a *sub-clinical* effect – damage to the body that has no obvious effect. But often, this sub-clinical damage accumulates over time until some sort of disease becomes detectable.

Allergens of almost every type create some negative response in the body, and most of those responses involve some sort of inflammation. It may be below detectable levels, but it's still there, weakening your body moment by moment. It should be fairly obvious that having fewer allergens in your environment is better than having more of them. It's certainly better for your overall health to have fewer allergens in your body creating less inflammation.

There are several problems with having chronic inflammation in your body. Chronic inflammation weakens your body's tissues, making them more susceptible to illnesses or diseases – like cancers. It also leads to your body forming scar tissue, and growing scar tissue will always reduce that tissue's ability to do its proper job - whether that scar tissue is in a muscle or an organ. Chronic inflammation also has more subtle effects that can affect your disposition and the people around you.

One of the most insidious is *irritation* – the emotional equivalent of inflammation. When you have underlying inflammation, your body is producing biochemicals that also affect your mood. When we inwardly feel more irritable, stress affects us more and we tend to have shorter "fuses." Because of this effect, and the chronic inflammation, it is much better for your health to get away from as many allergens as possible – whether they create observable effects, or the effects remain sub-clinical.

This may mean changing things you use at home, talking to your co-workers about the health benefits of eliminating chemical fragrances or burning candles, and may even mean moving to a different part of the country without the allergens and chemicals that are causing you harm.

Our environment

Our environment is not a huge static sponge that can absorb anything we spew into it. We've begun to learn that, and we're all experiencing the price of our collective short-sightedness. Plus, our situation is going to get worse before it gets better due to all the things we've already set in motion.

While this is a huge collective problem, it's also an immediate problem for every one of us – and our children and grandchildren. Thinking that only monumental efforts can make an important difference is as short-sighted as the choices we made to create the problem. Regardless of how enormous the problem is, *every tiny step makes a real difference – and each tiny step is important.*

I say this because every single one of us has the opportunity to make our immediate environment more in tune with nature, more healthful, and more sustainable. Some people are already doing this, and that trend is growing. In a sense, it's like a grass-roots effort to heal the Earth one small plot at a time.

As we pollute our immediate environment less, we're making our personal space on the planet healthier and better able to sustain our lives. After we pollute less, we can find ways to make better use of our resources. We can then become more knowledgeable stewards who help to heal the land and are rewarded by bounty and sustenance from the earth.

The principles of this type of stewardship are used in *permaculture,* and there are many excellent books available from which you can learn these principles. Some of them are likely to be in your local library, so you can learn about these principles without the expense of having to build a substantial library.

Something important to understand is that living a low-impact lifestyle in harmony with nature is very uplifting to someone on a spiritual journey – and particularly if you are seeking what is commonly called "enlightenment." A significant part of enlightenment is understanding that our relationship with each other and our planet is more than symbiotic.

It's more than that because we all ultimately are parts of the same, single consciousness that fills our universe. Living in harmony with the Earth, and with the Evolving Divine Consciousness, is an extraordinary spiritual attainment that we can all reach during this very lifetime.

The shift in perspective needed to achieve this is, at least to me, comparatively small. All that's needed is to acknowledge we've all done harm, and for each person to take responsibility for their personal impact on the planet from this point forward. Once we do this, every step we take brings us a step closer to this goal.

You'll see the results of taking responsibility for your personal impact when you can look around you and feel the holiness and harmony your attention and effort has brought to your space. Be an example, and help others do the same.

If we all do this to the best of our ability, we'll be healing ourselves as we heal the Earth. We'll be teaching future generations how to live in harmony with our planet once again. We can teach them how to preserve the Earth and its natural abundance, and how to share that abundance with each other and every other species in the world.

It will take time, many generations to be sure, but the price of *not* taking the first step is to never start this journey. If we collectively continue on our current course, and never start this healing journey, we and the Earth will perish before our natural time. That's why it's critical for each of us to start doing what we can. The choice is up to you and me, and I've chosen to become a proper steward for our land; to become an example that may benefit others. What do you choose?

Thoughts on fixing our social and governmental problems

Apathy and complacency in American society have led to some serious problems – problems that will need wisdom, vision, and hard work for several generations to overcome. We have collectively allowed greedy and corrupt politicians and corporate CEO's to rape and plunder our resources, and devastate this country and our world. This can be changed, but it has to start with the American people since the profiteers will not willingly give up their positions of power and ill-gotten gains.

Our corrupt government, composed of greedy politicians, corrupt lawyers, and greedy, corrupt corporate CEO's, MUST be replaced by Statesmen. Statesmen operate for the good of the country and the people in it. They're not swayed by greed, and cannot be bought off. They know that this country can only prosper when all of its citizens prosper. They know that we all need to collectively take an active part in operating our country according to these three fundamental guiding principles: 1) Do what you agree to do, 2) Respect other people's points of view, and 3) Respect other people's property.

In order for this to happen, it's vital that people with unimpeachable integrity do something they probably won't want to do: seek public office. That's the only real way to make a difference. We already know that making appeals for positive changes to a corrupt government won't create any meaningful change at all. We need to replace nearly all the politicians on Capitol Hill with Statesmen – from the President on down. That's the only way we'll be able to restore a proper American government to this country.

This is in no way a partisan statement. It's instead an attempt to break the hold that corrupt career politicians have on our government, and return control to those who are willing to work for the American people. It's time to get rid of this bloated government that views Americans as mindless cash machine workers the government can exploit, control and manipulate. It's time to pare down the government to its essential roles, and eliminate the "Big Brother" mentality in our current government.

The government is too big and too pervasive
It's obvious that our current government is severely ill and will destroy this country if allowed to continue on its current course. In my opinion, the current American government has shown itself to be a "collectivist" government, and that should *never* have happened in this country.

A "collectivist" government concentrates all the power and control into itself, robbing the population of all self-responsibility. This is in direct opposition to a spiritual perspective – in which each individual bears responsibility for their lives and actions. Because of this direct opposition, a collectivist government can never support true spiritual growth. Unfortunately, this is exactly what the government in the U.S. has become.

Our bloated government dictates and controls far too much of our lives, and I believe this is due at least in part to complacency. Too many Americans have lived behind blinders thinking, "Everything is more or less OK," and "What can we do about it anyway?"

It's time to drop away the blinders and to return the government to its true form: that of a Republic. In a republic, the supreme power rests in the *hands of the citizens,* and is *exercised* by their representatives. At a quick glance, and to refute my next assertion, I'm sure any member of our current government will say that a Republic is indeed what we have here in the United States. I say they're wrong.

I say the supreme power in this country resides in the *government,* and not the citizens. Time and time again, over decades, the government has eroded our personal control in our own lives against the wishes of many citizens. We're no longer the "land of the free." Instead, the U.S. has become the "land of what the government allows us to do."

If this country was indeed a republic, we would still have the freedoms allowed by our Constitution, rather than the handful of liberties those freedoms have been cut down to. This is because, in a republic, the primary role of the government is to safeguard its citizens, their rights, and their freedoms.

We, the American people, have allowed our government to become collectivist by our complacency. The Washington war machine that is our current government has the power now, but we can turn the tide back to prosperity, security, and personal responsibility – if enough of us stand up and take action. It will take decades, but the price of not doing so is to pass a bloated, weakened, dying government on to our children, grandchildren and *their* grandchildren – if it lasts that long. We'll be passing down a government that will continue to rain down destruction until it falls.

A bloated, ineffective government is an anchor on our country – an anchor on a very short chain that's threatening to pull our ship under. Remember that operating the government costs a tremendous amount of money, and *it does not produce value or wealth. It saps it.*

Instead of putting our resources into saving a doomed and sinking ship, let's use our energy to rebuild one stronger than ever before. If we get the right Statesmen in the right government positions, we'll be able to build our new vessel and even evacuate the old one before it sinks. Patching will no longer work. It's time to restructure.

Here are a few simple, common-sense ideas that will go a long way to help us and future generations. These aren't new ideas, and they can be relatively easily done – once we break the death grip the corrupt politicians have on our government.

1) Eliminate career politics. Every office should be temporary and have limits that cannot be exceeded. It should be possible for any qualified American to become elected to a suitable position. One way to make this more feasible would be to eliminate the current hurdles that exist for independent candidates to get on ballots. Perhaps we could form an election bureau that would oversee the process of ensuring a candidate meets the job qualifications before running for office.

2) Eliminate the political party system and the stranglehold they have on the election process. At this point in our history, the party system is only useful to the status quo – the greedy and corrupt who are already in power. Eliminating the party system would also eliminate their grip on our government.

3) Reduce the reach and size of the government so it can be sustainably funded by the revenue generated

by the citizens of this country.

4) Operate the government within its budget. This should have been a no-brainer, but the greedy politicians no doubt saw a way to fatten their kitty once the need for war deficit spending had passed. Statesmen would have stopped the excess spending, knowing that they would be stealing from the American public if they didn't.

5) Simplify the tax code to a graduated flat tax. This can be fairly easily done, and will generate enough revenue to operate the government, along with other *appropriate and specific taxes* – especially once the extreme bloat is pared away.

6) Eliminate the socialized medicine "scheme" enacted by the Obama administration. The solution to the medical insurance problem in this country needs to begin with tort reform and reducing excessive awards, which have led to excessive "CYA" medical testing as the norm to satisfy legal requirements. I believe that removing the extreme and unrealistic accountability required of physicians today will be enough to bring health insurance costs down considerably, and good insurance will be available to almost all Americans at a reasonable price.

More than these six will ultimately need to be done, and I'm sure that many people have some other great ideas to help fix this mess. Starting with these will be enough to keep us busy for quite a while, and, more importantly, these ideas will also provide short-term positive improvements for all Americans.

How to deepen your spiritual understanding

Deepening your spiritual understanding comes about one small shift in perspective at a time with only occasional large shifts, if any. It's not a process that requires a person to retire from "worldly" life and live in austerity and solitude. True spiritual understanding can, and does, unfold from our hectic, everyday lives. As it is *right now*, your life is a perfect vehicle for developing a deeper spiritual perspective.

This comes about mainly through shifting your *perception*. What you perceive, and how you process that perception, is an important part of shifting your perspective to one that is more spiritual. The events you experience every day contain all the content you need to develop a true and deep spiritual perspective. So how can each of us change our perception to become more aware of the spiritual content in our everyday lives?

The process is fairly simple, and it starts with recognizing our *habitual* response patterns. Over time, we've developed patterns of response to the events around us. This makes life easier in a few ways. Habitual responses serve to decrease stress, because we have an immediate and ready response to almost any action we encounter during our day. Response patterns save us mental effort from having to think of a response. They also reduce fear, since this event is no longer an unknown and has, from our point of view, an immediate way to resolve it.

Here is a personal example of a habitual response: I get irritated when I see people do stupid things when they clearly know better. That response really makes no sense, but it's been difficult for me to eliminate. If you think back to the section on negative emotions, you'll remember that irritation often comes about when the world doesn't conform to what we want it to be.

The reason my irritation response makes no sense is twofold; 1) Ironically, I know better; and 2) The world is under no obligation to conform to what I want. My reaction still happens sometimes despite knowing those things. It's something I still want to outgrow – and hopefully soon!

Once we recognize our habitual responses, it's important to examine them as they arise. It's important to understand *why* we responded that way, and to identify the specific benefit we get from that response. After that, the next step is to think about and look for other factors that could exist that you may not be aware of. Think about *how* this situation came to be exactly as it is, and *why* it is the way it is. Then consider how these newly uncovered factors influence your choice of reaction.

Next, determine if your habitual reaction is the *best possible* reaction to that event. If not, what choice would be better? Is there a reason you *can't* make that choice and change your response? If you find a reason to not change your response, is that reason actually just rationalizing your habitual response?

I know that may seem like lot to go through, but following this process will help you to ferret out and eliminate habitual responses that you no longer need and that are holding you back from greater progress. Taking a short time to apply this process helps to teach you the process of looking for the deeper truths that are often buried in every situation. This process also lets you look deeply at yourself, and offers you the opportunity for growth and change during almost every moment of your current daily life.

Over time, you'll develop the "habit" of looking more deeply into things and looking for the spiritual lesson contained in each event of our lives. Once this shift occurs and you develop this habit, you're effectively deepening your perspective and spiritual understanding every day while living your daily life. This leads to a greater understanding of the concept that the universe has only one single consciousness, and brings your awareness closer each day to that consciousness. It's a cycle that builds to create a very specific result.

What can we individually become?

The result is that each of us eventually becomes a living, breathing manifestation of the ever-unfolding Evolving Divine Consciousness. Once this happens, this Divinely manifested part of us is in control of our lives, and our ego (the part of our mind that sees us as an individual) essentially "translates" Divine Intention into a form our mind can understand. And, if appropriate, the ego can help bring this Divine Intention into physical manifestation.

Although being in direct contact with God may seem like something that only happens rarely and generally to someone else, it's important to recognize that, while we're all at different points on the path, we're all traveling the *same* path.

This means that every one of us can be in direct contact with God. Will we all achieve this from just having read this book? Unfortunately not. However, I firmly believe that coming to a deep understanding of what I've presented will speed up your spiritual growth a great deal.

It's my hope that you'll be able to travel more of the path than you would have without having read this book. Believing that it is possible, and can happen to you, is an essential step and makes it much more likely to happen in this lifetime.

What is beyond the universe?

The simple answer is this: the universe where our creator lives. This is the level of existence where energy is actually created. This created energy is then gathered and infused with a spiritual consciousness, and combining these two is how each universe comes into being.

The structure is somewhat similar to how our eyes are constructed. Think of our universe as the eye, and the center of our universe – the enormous black hole – is like

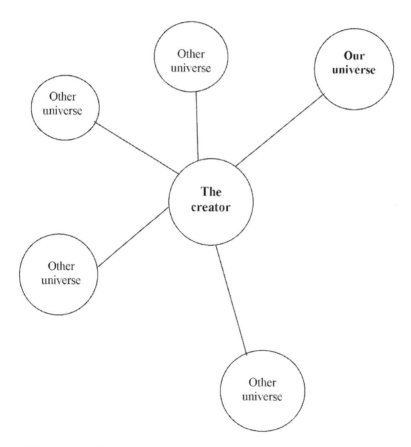

The creator of our universe has created other universes too. Each of them connects to the creator in the same way ours does. Other creators exist as well, with universes of their own creation.

the optic disk, but imagine it's right in the middle of the eye. There's a bidirectional connection similar to the optic nerve, and it's connected to the source of all consciousness, our creator – which equates to our physical brain.

Our universe isn't the only one our creator has brought into being. There are at least dozens of others, and there are other creators too.

The physics in our universe don't include any description of how to create energy, and can't explain how to create it. At the creation level of existence, our creator simply harnessed the created energy and infused that energy with consciousness to create a distinct entity – the Evolving Divine Consciousness of our universe.

In a sense, this act also created a duality that some have described as Father/God, Mother/Goddess. In this paradigm, the Father/God is the Creator, and the Mother/Goddess is the Evolving Divine Consciousness.

Once this energy became infused with pure consciousness, our universe experienced the Big Bang. As a side note, this means that every bit of energy and matter in our universe – even the tiniest bit – contains consciousness.

This energy is created beyond our universe, and I can't tell you the exact way energy is created there. However, I do know that the process is similar to generating static electricity here on earth. Essentially, friction between moving molecules creates static electricity in our universe. But in the universe outside of ours – the realm of our universe's creator – that same process of friction seems to create energy and not static electricity.

Unfortunately, I don't know any more than that about

creating energy right now. Perhaps at some time in our future one or more of us will have the capability of learning more about the process that creates energy – hopefully *much* more. I am certain, however, that our knowledge will continue to grow and expand as we collectively become more spiritually aware.

Goals from reading this book

It's impossible for me to know why a specific reader is interested in this book, and exactly what they're looking for. With that being said, there are some goals I want to achieve with most readers.

1) To open your mind to the idea of greater possibilities; possibilities that redefine our view of our universe and bring a sense of definitive purpose to our existence.
2) To pique your curiosity. This book presents an overview of several vast topics, and I'm hoping you'll be inspired to explore some or all of these concepts in greater depth.
3) To reduce stress and negative feelings in your life. Truly internalizing these concepts can help you to know, at a deep level, that everything in your life and around you has meaning. This perspective will help you move past the anxiety and anguish of uncertainty.
4) To help you reach your full spiritual potential in this lifetime. This book can be a doorway for you; a doorway into a realm you may not have known existed, but perhaps hoped that it did. I welcome the opportunity to help you walk through that doorway and to help you on the path beyond.

I'd like to do a bit more to help your spiritual growth. I've set up a small forum at www.kevinadam.com to answer as many of your questions as I can. I won't be able to answer every question personally if the book gets very popular, but by then we'll be forming a solid community of spiritually aware people, and other readers can help answer questions. We'll have the opportunity to learn from each other.

I know that I don't have all the answers, and my readers

have things to teach me, too. It's a part of our spiritual journeys that we can share, and every person added to our group makes us stronger and more able to create positive change.

When you get to the website, you'll see a tab on the menu called "Book Forum." Click that link to go to the forum page. Introduce yourself first if you'd like, and ask your question. Remember that this is a new forum, so the first visitors will be the first posters. Hope to see you there.

Kevin

Resources

These are some resources that I've found helpful, and you may too. You'll notice that some of these resources have complex Internet links. I want you to know that I'll get a small commission if you use these links to make a purchase. Your cost won't change, and you're naturally not under any obligation to use these links, but I'd be grateful if you did.

These resources will lead you to others, and remember to visit www.kevinadam.com if you have questions. Thank you for allowing me to join you on this journey of spiritual awakening.

Human energy field
Myss, Caroline: *The Anatomy of Spirit*
http://www.amazon.com/gp/product/0609800140/ref=
copy038-20

Brennan, Barbara: *Hands of Light*
http://www.amazon.com/gp/product/0553345397/ref=
copy038-20

Learning meditation
www.integralenlightenment.com

Permaculture
Shein, Christopher: *Vegetable Gardener's Guide to Permaculture*
http://www.amazon.com/gp/product/1604692707/ref=
copy038-20

Jacke, Toensmeier: *Edible Forest Gardens*
http://www.amazon.com/gp/product/1890132608/ref=
copy038-20

Reich, Lee: *Landscaping with Fruit*
http://www.amazon.com/gp/product/1603420916/ref=
copy038-20

Mollison, Bill: *Introduction to Permaculture*
http://www.amazon.com/gp/product/0908228082/ref=
copy038-20

Natural Home Building
Chiras, Daniel: *The Natural House*
http://www.amazon.com/gp/product/1890132578/ref=
copy038-20

The New Ecological Home
http://www.amazon.com/gp/product/1931498164/ref= copy038-
20

The Solar House
http://www.amazon.com/gp/product/1931498121/ref= copy038-
20

Power from the Sun
http://www.amazon.com/gp/product/0865716218/ref= copy038-
20

Matesz, Ken: *Masonry Heaters*
http://www.amazon.com/gp/product/1603582134/ref= copy038-
20

Water Conservation
Downey, Nate: *Harvest the Rain*
http://www.amazon.com/gp/product/0865344957/ref= copy038-
20

Self-Protection
Target Focus Training
https://m260.infusionsoft.com/go/TFT/adamk999/

Soap making supplies
www.bulkapothacary.com

26919874R00069

Made in the USA
Charleston, SC
24 February 2014